CLONMACNOISE STUDIES

VOL. 1

Clonmacnoise Studies

Vol. 1
Seminar Papers 1994

Edited by Heather A. King

AN ROINN COMHSHAOIL, OIDHREACHTA AGUS RIALTAIS ÁITIÚIL

DEPARTMENT OF THE ENVIRONMENT, HERITAGE
AND LOCAL GOVERNMENT

Cover: Aerial view of Clonmacnoise (photo: Con Brogan)
Cover design: Geraldine Garland

ISBN 978-0-7076-5098-2

British Library Cataloguing-in-Publication Data.
A catalogue record for this book is available from the British Library.

First published in 1998
Dúchas, The Heritage Service
51 St Stephen's Green.

Reprinted in 2007
Department of the Environment, Heritage and Local Government
Dún Sceine
Harcourt Lane
Dublin 2

Typeset in Ireland by Wordwell Ltd.
Origination by Wordwell Ltd and the Type Bureau.

Printed by Castuera, Pamplona

Future volumes in this series:
Volume 2: The early medieval bridge at Clonmacnoise
Volume 3: Seminar papers 1998
Volume 4: Excavations at the high crosses
Volume 5: Archaeological excavations at Clonmacnoise

Contents

Foreword

It is now four years since Heather King organised a one-day conference at Clonmacnoise, that most evocative of archaeological sites. Clonmacnoise Studies Vol. 1 is the fruit of that pleasant and lively day of debate and happily there will be other days and other books devoted to the subject. These essays are a pleasure to read. The authors in most cases have given short summaries of new work. Some — the reports on the excavations near the National School by Raghnall Ó Floinn and Heather King and the coins by Michael Kenney are complete statements. The masterly account of the Cathedral by Conleth Manning may be taken as definitive. He makes a persuasive case for identifying the earliest part of the fabric with the church built in 909 by King Flann Sinna and Abbot Colmán. He charts the subsequent history of the building with great skill by a study of the masonry and by careful use of old records. The contributions of Peter Harbison and of John Scarry enrich our knowledge of the Clonmacnoise archive. Harbison identifies four watercolour drawings of the monuments by Beranger while Scarry documents the early photographs of the site many of them containing valuable information about the state of the monuments in the last century. Both remind us of the place Clonmacnoise came to occupy in the imagination and of how that imagination was fed by illustrations in tour guides and early scholarly publications.

Clonmacnoise became important symbolically not merely because it was 'marketed' in eighteenth- and nineteenth-century tourist literature but also because it was important in ancient times. This importance was due to a complex of factors, spiritual and temporal. Its siting, not in a howling wilderness but at the centre of converging routes, by land, along eskers, and by water along the Shannon, was clearly critical. Aonghus Moloney describes in detail the number of timber and gravel causeways leading towards Clonmacnoise which served pilgrims, traders and other travellers and connected valuable islands of dry land as the peat bogs of the area expanded. The early medieval bridge at Clonmacnoise recently discovered emphasises the place as a nexus of communication. Mary Tubridy's description of the environment before the monastery was founded reminds us just how much the landscape in the area had been modified by human activity since Neolithic times — a process which continued and probably intensified with the growth of the ecclesiastical site and its dependencies. Annette Kehnel gives a sample of her attempt (definitively published elsewhere) to reconstruct the land-holdings of ancient Clonmacnoise. Her work is a welcome attempt to add precision to speculation about the economy of the foundation. It drew on the production of many widely scattered holdings. Nancy Edwards and Raghnall Ó Floinn deal in different ways with the artistic output of the Church of Ciarán, reflecting on that wealth in another way. Changing patterns of patronage make it clear that Clonmacnoise was not insulated from the political world as an earlier generation of scholarship might have implied, and the interest of leading dynasties brought significant donations to it in the eleventh and twelfth centuries.

John Bradley contributes a thoughtful paper on Clonmacnoise as a monastic town, in which he shows how similar its layout was to Armagh and, probably, Tuam and Kells. No accident this, he suggests that 'the concept of an ideal monastic town plan existed in the minds of the authorities responsible for its layout'. Whether that ideal was a worldly or a spiritual one would be a fruitful line of enquiry.

Dr Michael Ryan
Director, Chester Beatty Library

Preface

Little did I realise, when I arrived in Clonmacnoise in the early summer of 1990 to work as a site supervisor for my colleague, Con Manning, that I would spend every summer of the following nine years excavating on this very special monastic site. 1990 was the beginning for me of a love affair with Clonmacnoise which has grown stronger with each season's new discoveries.

Clonmacnoise means many things to many people and few visitors go away disappointed, even on a day when a grey blanket of rain comes sheeting in from the west to envelop the site or when the east wind whips across the top of the esker ridge, forcing one to seek shelter beside unroofed walls. There is always something magical about the place, especially if one is fortunate enough to be there early on a summer's morning and see and hear a pair of swans sweep in across the Shannon to feed along the shore, or to stand beside the west door of the Cathedral on an autumn evening and watch the sun sink behind the Cross of the Scriptures. There is balm for the soul and calm from the stresses of our modern world.

A romantic view of the site was also recorded by Angus O'Gillan in the first verse of his poem *Clonmacnoise,* translated from Irish by T.W. Roleston (1857–1920):

'In a quiet water'd land, a land of roses,
Stands Saint Kieran's city fair
And the warriors of Erin in their famous generations
Slumber there'.

One gets the impression from the poem of a town long abandoned but with visible reminders of its one-time greatness as a 'city' and as a burial-place for many of the great historical figures of Ireland. The multitudes of visitors who throng the site today, particularly during the summer months, probably go away with an image of the 'quiet water'd land' in which the ruins of Saint Ciarán's monastery still stand, while the high crosses and the large numbers of cross-slabs indicate the importance of the site as a religious centre and burial-place, but I think it is probably difficult during the average two-hour visit to imagine the busy bustling town Clonmacnoise would have been in its heyday. The buildings, deserted and roofless now, are just the more enduring remains of the ecclesiastical core of the site. There is so much more that is not visible but which is documented in the annals and has now been uncovered through excavation and survey.

St Ciarán's decision to found a monastery in the middle of the sixth century on an important crossing-point in the centre of Ireland where the Shannon meets the Slí Mhór on the Eiscir Riada was no mere accident. The strategic importance of this location was undoubtedly one of the factors that caused the monastery to flourish. Within a year of its foundation there were at least two churches on the site; there was an enclosure and the beginnings of pilgrimage in the seventh century. Raids in the eighth century by the Irish and Viking attacks in the early ninth suggest a settlement worth robbing, while the erection of crosses and stone churches in the ninth and tenth centuries speak of wealthy patronage. The annals also recount the building of roads and the existence of a bridge in the eleventh and twelfth centuries. Some of this information is verifiable by looking at the site today, but references, such as that in the early thirteenth century, to 135 houses being burned forces one to look around the deserted fields today and wonder where they were located.

The excitement of the last ten years has been that the results of the excavations on land and underwater, together with field-walking on newly ploughed fields and geophysical survey, have been unfolding the truth of the picture painted in the annals. A nucleus of settlement on the banks of the Shannon expanded between the sixth and twelfth centuries into a large town extending from the Nuns' Church on the east to the site of the castle on the west, with a wooden bridge in the early ninth century linking the east and west of Ireland. The thirteenth century saw a decline in the fortunes of the site and it is from the following centuries that one might more correctly describe the monastery as being situated in a 'quiet water'd land'. The Normans were driven out shortly after they had built their castle, the church was re-organised and Clonmacnoise faded into relative obscurity. It is, however, fortunate that it did not develop throughout the centuries into a modern town, as the continued occupation of sites such as Armagh has destroyed the evidence for early medieval settlement. As it is, the remains of a thriving bustling town lie undamaged in the fields along the Eiscir Riada. This has meant that when an archaeologist puts a trowel into the ground one is immediately brought back to the stratified deposits of the late twelfth or early thirteenth century. The gravelled roads and streets, round and rectangular houses, open-air hearths for cooking and metal-working, workshops and kilns, together with the artefacts of the people who lived and worked in Clonmacnoise, have been recovered.

During the excavations there has been a constant stream of foreign and Irish tourists, visiting scholars and particularly local visitors to the site, who were always amazed at the wealth of artefacts uncovered. While I constantly reassured people that it was incumbent upon me to publish the results of my work, I was struck on one occasion by the remark that all of this information would be published in some obscure journal and that lectures would be given in foreign places or 'up in Dublin', and that the present-day inhabitants of Clonmacnoise would never get the opportunity to learn more about their native place. It was with this challenge in mind and with the realisation that there was a genuine thirst for knowledge about the site that the first Clonmacnoise seminar came about. It was held in a packed Temple Connor, and the enthusiasm from speakers and audience was such that it was clear that the event should not be allowed to fade away. The seminar proceedings developed into this publication and are presented here as Volume 1 of a series that will, in the future, carry the papers presented at the 1998 seminar, and will include a volume on the discovery of the medieval bridge and a number of volumes on the excavations of the high crosses, at the Visitor Centre and in the New Graveyard.

It is my hope that this series, devoted exclusively to the study of all things pertinent to Clonmacnoise, will, in a small way, repay the hospitality that I have received and give something back to Clonmacnoise for the many happy years that I have spent working there. I hope also that the series will lead many more people to understand, protect and cherish this very special monastic site.

Heather A. King

Acknowledgements

It is with pleasure that I express my gratitude to the many people who have helped to bring this publication about. Firstly I would like to thank the contributors, who were all enthusiastic supporters of the 1994 seminar and willingly agreed, and in some cases suggested, that the papers should be published. The seminar could not have been held without support from the staff of the National Monuments Service. In particular I would like to record my thanks to Con Manning, and the (then) Chief Archaeologist Peter Danagher. My thanks also to the Rev. Martha Greystack, who kindly allowed us the use of Temple Connor, to my own staff, Donald and Deirdre Murphy, Kieran Norton, Liam Darcy, Pat Anderson, Laura Claffey and Karen Higgins, the Manager, Tom Moore, and the guiding staff on the site who provided all the back-up preparation for the day. The publication could not have been achieved without the support of the present Chief Archaeologist, David Sweetman, and the administrative back-up of Declan Ford and Tom Fitzgerald. I am doubly grateful to several of my colleagues in National Monuments for reading the various papers: David Sweetman, Con Manning, Colmán Ó Críodáin and Dr Ann Lynch, who made many constructive comments. Mary Tunney's expertise in layout and presentation and the illustrations by Gerry Woods are acknowledged. The photographic staff, Con Brogan, John Scarry and especially Tony Roche, were unendingly helpful. My thanks to Michael Ryan who, despite his onerous workload, has kindly written the foreword and been wonderfully supportive of the project. I would also like to record my gratitude to the library staff of the Royal Irish Academy, the Royal Society of Antiquaries, the photographic sections of the National Library of Ireland and of the Ulster Museum. Raghnall Ó Floinn was agreeable to having his paper, originally published in a volume entitled *From the Isles of the North*, reprinted here, and I am grateful to the editor, Cormac Bourke, and HMSO for their permission to do so. Likewise Michael Kenny gave permission for his paper on the Clonmacnoise coin hoard, which was originally printed in the *Numismatic Society of Ireland Occasional Papers,* to be reproduced here. I am happy to acknowledge the kindness of Dr Roe FitzGerald in giving me her slides of the natural environment around Clonmacnoise which illustrate Mary Tubridy's paper and of Conor McDermot in the Irish Archaeological Wetland Unit for providing Ill. 2 for Aonghus Moloney's paper. Finally, a very large thank you to the staff at Wordwell, Nick Maxwell, Emer Condit and especially Jen Brady, who have worked so hard to see these papers through to publication.

1. THE PRE-MONASTIC ENVIRONMENT AT CLONMACNOISE

Mary Tubridy

Ill. 1—Clonmacnoise from the east (photo: Dúchas, The Heritage Service).

Introduction

When visitors arrive at Clonmacnoise they are always impressed by the landscape of the monument—the river and callows and the low hills or eskers (Ill. 1). They see a pristine landscape, they revel in its tranquillity, and they feel comfortable with the gentle scale of the topography and the human settlement pattern.

The landscape in the immediate vicinity of Clonmacnoise is of intrinsic importance for nature conservation (Ill. 2). It contains habitats which are rare elsewhere in Ireland and Europe and which survive here owing to the less intensive scale of development. From 1981 to 1988 the EU funded research projects which examined farming, wildlife conservation and special interest tourism in the area immediately around Clonmacnoise. This work has been written up in a series of reports (Tubridy 1984; 1987; 1989; Jeffrey 1986) produced for the EU, and in a book for the general public, *The Heritage of Clonmacnoise* (Tubridy and Jeffrey 1987), which was published with the assistance and support of local and national agencies.

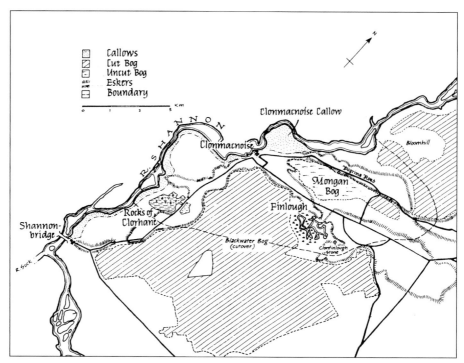

Ill. 2—Clonmacnoise Heritage Zone (drawing: Harry McConville).

Ill. 3—Esker grassland (photo: Roe FitzGerald).

As one of the important criteria for ranking sites of nature conservation importance is 'naturalness', the history of the landscape around Clonmacnoise has been intensively studied. This report describes what is now known about the landscape in the prehistoric period.

Eskers

The monastery is situated on an 'esker', a low ridge above the floodplain of the Shannon. The geographical term 'esker' is derived from the Irish word *eiscir*, meaning sand and gravel hill. The midlands are criss-crossed by eskers of varying heights and orientations which were formed in streams under the melting ice-cap at the end of the last Ice Age. As this landscape is relatively flat, excellent views are obtained from the summits of the eskers. The esker on which the monastery is situated was called the *Eiscir Riada* or *Slí Mhór* ('important routeway') as it was an east–west transport route during the Early Christian period. The section of the *Eiscir Riada* to the east of the monastery is still known as the 'Pilgrim's Road' (Ills 2 and 4).

The first farmers in Clonmacnoise found a

Ill. 4—Pilgrim's Road (photo: Heather A. King).

mixed woodland with oak, elm and hazel on the eskers. Some of this was cleared before the monastic period, so that by the time the monastery was founded most of the eskers were covered in grassland. The fields which developed on eskers were used for winter grazing. They were naturally dry and fertile and allowed for the growth of grass later in the season.

In fields on steep-sided slopes one can still see the plants which evolved under this gentle clearance and grazing regime. Their steepness has preserved the fields from ploughing and excessive use of fertiliser, and as a result many still have a species-rich semi-natural grassland which reflects the original soil and natural topography. Some of the flowering plants are particularly attractive. Orchids, creeping wild thyme, carline thistle, quaking grass and large daisies can be seen in many fields, particularly those on steep-sided and south-facing slopes (Ill. 3). This display contrasts with the appearance of fields in intensively managed farming areas, which comprise sown grasses and clovers. The presence of these species suggests not only that these grasslands are ancient but that they have continued to be managed in ways which have preserved their naturalness.

Mongan Bog

On the other side of the esker on which the monastery was built is Mongan Bog (Ill. 5). This small raised bog (owned by An Taisce) is one of a few relatively intact raised bogs in Ireland. Bogland once covered 70% of County Offaly but drainage and large-scale peat-cutting have fatally damaged most bogs. Mongan Bog has been growing over the last 3500 years, and its centre has changed little since the time of the monastic settlement. It is still a wet spongy mass of peat which is dangerous for people and animals. During the period of use of the monastery there was a natural drain called a 'lagg' around this bog which drained the bog and surrounding eskers. Drainage, turf-cutting and reclamation have resulted in the disappearance of this wetland.

Callows

The land along the banks of the Shannon is called 'callows'. It is naturally fertile, as winter and summer flooding deposits silt in the fields.

The natural vegetation of callows was

Ill. 5—Mongan Bog (photo: Mary Tubridy).

3

a fen woodland dominated by willow and alder (Tubridy 1989). When this woodland was cleared, it was gradually replaced by a diverse grassland comprising species that tolerate flooding. While most of the callow land bordering the Shannon is used for grazing, the callows to the north-west of the monastery is unusual in being used solely for hay-making. Documentary records confirm that hay-making has taken place there since the eighteenth century. Hay is always saved late in the summer. This is usually compatible with the use of the site by the now rare corncrake, which is able to raise its young before the grass is cut. Hay-making is a preferred land use for wildlife conservation as the soil is not disturbed by trampling animals, and plants are allowed to set seed.

In winter the Shannon in the midlands is transformed into a 6500ha shallow lake supporting internationally important populations of migratory geese and swans. These must have been an important source of food for the monastery.

Fin Lough

Fin Lough is a shallow lake situated between the northern margin of the drained and exploited Blackwater Bog and the *Eiscir Riada*. It is a vivid reminder of the landscape that dominated the midlands and Clonmacnoise between 9000 and 3500 years ago. At this time the shallow basins which now comprise the Shannon margins and bogs were filled with shallow lakes. Rushes, sedges, reeds, willows and later alder grew around them. Salmon, eels, ducks, geese and swans were common (Ill. 6).

Unlike other shallow lakes, Fin Lough did not grow into an acid raised bog. Its existence has been maintained by inputs of alkaline water from the surrounding eskers and groundwater sources. Over the last 7000 years it has been an open wetland, occupying more or less the same location along the northern edge of the cut and drained Blackwater Bog.

Fin Lough is important for wildlife as it contains a diverse range of habitats and species. Habitats include a fen/bog transition and a small birch woodland on acid peat. Extensive field studies have revealed the importance of the reedswamp and fen for rare moths and beetles. The fauna includes teal, tufted duck and coot, as well as pike, perch, rudd, minnow and sticklebacks. A decline in the population of wetland birds and the absence of migratory fish are almost certainly due to a decrease in the area of open water caused by drainage.

The basin has been drained over the last 150 years, initially in connection with farming but in the last 50 years in association with the exploitation of the adjoining Blackwater Bog.

Ill. 6—Fin Lough (photo: Mary Tubridy).

Ill. 7—'The Rocks' of Clorhane (photo: Heather A. King).

As a result, plants are now taking over more of the lake, and each year there is less open water. An area which was familiar to the first people who came to Clonmacnoise is in imminent danger of disappearing.

'The Rocks' of Clorhane

On the road from Clonmacnoise to Shannonbridge, between the esker and the Shannon, is an expanse of limestone pavement known locally as 'The Rocks' (Ill. 7). From research in the Burren it is likely that 'The Rocks' supported an oak, ash and elm woodland at the time of the earliest farmers. Since then the vegetation cover has fluctuated between grassland, woodland and scrub, depending on management.

Maps reveal the presence of woodland in the seventeenth century. By the nineteenth century this had been cleared, and the area was used for rough grazing. The relaxation of grazing since then has allowed a particularly dense hazel scrub to appear, which was partially underplanted by conifers in the 1940s. The hazel branches are clothed in dense growths of mosses and lichens. Clearings in the hazel commonly have colourful grasslands featuring large anthills. Plants of interest here include the orchid species found on the eskers. Buckthorn, commonly associated with limestone pavement in the Burren, is found on the pavement. An interesting feature of the flora at the site is the presence of a small population of regenerating yew, a native conifer which succeeded the oak/ash/elm woodland. This area may have been a source of stone as the limestone is near the surface and the proximity of the river would have allowed its transport by boat.

Conclusions

The area around Clonmacnoise is remarkable for the clues it offers to the earliest landscapes. These clues are of interest to archaeologists and historians, to ecologists studying habitats which retain significant natural features, and to visitors who wish to understand the particular nature of the relationship between man and the environment. They have been intensively studied because of their importance for nature conservation, and there is potential for further research into the relationship between archaeology and landscape conservation.

It is vitally important that a coordinated management system be established which recognises the special quality of the landscape around Clonmacnoise for archaeology, wildlife, landscape conservation and recreation. Such a system should be developed and managed in partnership with the natural guardians of the landscape—the landowners and the local community.

References

Jeffrey, D. 1986 The Clonmacnoise Heritage Zone: economic and social appraisal, interpretation and implementation. Report to the EEC under research contract 6613/84/017. Environmental Sciences Unit, Trinity College, Dublin.

Tubridy, M. 1984 Creation and management of a Heritage Zone at Clonmacnoise, Co. Offaly, Ireland. Report to the EEC under research contract 6612/12. Environmental Sciences Unit, Trinity College, Dublin.

Tubridy, M. (ed.) 1987 *Heritage Zones: the co-existence of agriculture, nature conservation and tourism*. Proceedings of a conference on the Clonmacnoise Heritage Zone, Tullamore, 29/30 October 1986. Environmental Sciences Unit, Trinity College, Dublin.

Tubridy, M. 1989 Clonmacnoise Heritage Zone Project. A portfolio of management plans. Report to the EEC under research contract 6611/85/08-1. Environmental Sciences Unit, Trinity College, Dublin.

Tubridy, M. and Jeffrey, D. (eds) 1987 *The Heritage of Clonmacnoise*. Environmental Sciences Unit, Trinity College, Dublin, and County Offaly Vocational Educational Committee.

2. FROM EAST AND WEST, CROSSING THE BOGS AT CLONMACNOISE

Aonghus Moloney

Ill. 1—Bogland to the north of Clonmacnoise (photo: Dúchas, The Heritage Service).

The monastic centre of Clonmacnoise is located in an area of extensive bogland (Ill. 1; see Tubridy, this vol., ills 1 and 2). Large raised bogs, divided and interspersed by eskers and isolated upland drumlins, form part of a chain of bogland which extends, on both sides of the River Shannon, from the town of Athlone in the north to beyond the town of Banagher to the south. Although the immediate area of the monastic centre is dominated by the Shannon and the esker on which it is situated, raised bogs extend beyond these on all sides.

Previously, it was often considered that these bogs formed an impenetrable barrier, confining access to Clonmacnoise to the chain of eskers or from the river itself. However, from early records of the archaeology of the area, and from the more recent work of the Irish Archaeological Wetland Unit (IAWU), it is now apparent that these large bogs need not have formed such impenetrable barriers as previously believed, and there is good evidence for the construction of toghers and gravel roads across many (IAWU 1995, 67–139). The stone 'Pilgrim's Road', which extends eastwards from the Nuns' Church along the esker referred to as Pike's Hill, has often been described as a togher, and may well have crossed a narrow area of bogland to the north-east of the now-preserved Mongan Bog (Moloney 1995, 5; IAWU 1995, 114–15).

The archaeological material found in these bogs covers a broad chronological range. Amongst the earliest sites were the Late Bronze Age settlement at Clonfinlough, Co. Offaly (IAWU 1993), and the large wooden togher found at Annaghcorrib, Co. Galway, also dating to the Later Bronze Age (Raftery *et al.* 1995). In all, the IAWU survey of the bogs in the Blackwater group, encircling Clonmacnoise, uncovered over 250 previously unrecorded sites, mainly gravel roads and wooden trackways. These indicated that communication across the bogs took place from prehistoric times until comparatively recently. Several of the sites may have been directly or indirectly associated with the monastic centre at Clonmacnoise.

The association of toghers or gravel roads with monastic centres is common throughout the midlands. Many of the earlier reported sites were known locally as 'Pilgrim's Road' or 'Monk's Path' and reputedly led to or from a local monastic centre. Although subsequent investigations of many of these toghers revealed that they often pre-dated the monastery in question by millennia, there nevertheless remains a strong tradition of association between toghers/gravel roads and monastic sites. For example, a gravel road, part of which still remains, was recorded to the south-west of Clonfert Cathedral (IAWU 1995, 85). Although the date of construction of this road is as yet unconfirmed, it has been traditionally associated with the ecclesiastical site, and remained in use until fairly recently.

Apart from the 'Pilgrim's Road' noted above, two other gravel roads are worthy of mention in connection with Clonmacnoise. These are the gravel road at Coolumber, Co. Roscommon, and the series of gravel roads in Bloomhill Bog, counties Offaly and Westmeath.

Ill. 2—Bloomhill road (photo: Irish Archaeological Wetland Unit).

Bloomhill Bog consists of several interconnecting raised mires which completely surround Bloomhill 'bog island', a dryland area to the north-east of Clonmacnoise (see Tubridy, this vol., ill. 2). During Bord na Móna drainage works to the north-east of the island, a large gravel road was discovered, running between the island and the north-eastern dryland at Ballynahownwood, Co. Westmeath. Sections of the gravel road were first excavated by Breen in 1983 and 1986 (Breen 1988). During the IAWU survey of the area in 1992, it became apparent that parts of the road were in imminent danger from the continuous peat-milling in the area, and so the Unit undertook a further investigation of a small section of the road (McDermott 1995).

Both Breen's and the IAWU's excavations uncovered a large gravel and flagstone roadway of complex composition, suggesting numerous construction and repair phases. The road appears to have been constructed and used between AD 566 and 770 (Breen 1988; calibrated in Moloney 1995, 18) and then intermittently until the second half of the thirteenth century. McDermott (1995, 66), in discussing the function of the road, suggests that it formed part of a broader pattern of routes throughout the area, with Clonmacnoise as one possible focal-point. The evidence from other bogs in the area tends to support this, and the area around Clonmacnoise may have been served by a series of major routeways. Both Breen and McDermott note that the road may have been one of several which extended from Bloomhill island to the surrounding dryland areas. In fact, the present road which links the island to the south is reputedly built on the line of, or directly over, an earlier gravel road.

The presence of a gravel road in Coolumber Bog, Co. Roscommon, came to light in 1983 when it was reported to the National Museum, although unconfirmed reports of its discovery during peat-cutting had been known locally for some time. At present, a section of the road is exposed at the north-eastern edge of the bog, and this was recorded by the IAWU during their survey of the area (1995, 119). The road runs in a north-east to south-west direction, directly below the modern road which leads from Nure village towards Clonmacnoise. Overall, it is similar in width (2.5m) to the Bloomhill road, although the complex layers of the latter are not present in the exposed section of the Coolumber road. The tradition of a road across the bogs in this area is maintained by the fact that the modern road is constructed along the same line as the earlier gravel road.

Although it was not possible to trace the easternmost extent of this gravel road, its direction indicated that it ran to the narrow area of 'callow' land on the western bank of the Shannon, almost directly opposite Clonmacnoise. The recent discovery of a wooden bridge by the Irish Underwater Archaeological Research Team (IUART) at Clonmacnoise (Moore 1996, 24–7) would seem to indicate that the gravel road at Coolumber may have been one of the main western approaches to the bridge and the monastic centre.

Tracing the line of the road from the nearest western dryland to the bank of the river indicates that over 2.2km of road would have been constructed over bog. The initial construction of such a road would have taken over 1600m^3 of gravel. As with the Bloomhill road (McDermott 1995, 65), the gravel and clay used in the Coolumber road could have been obtained from nearby glacial deposits but would still have required considerable effort and organisation. Given the size and importance of Clonmacnoise as a monastic centre, it is hardly surprising that such a gravel road, and wooden bridge, would be required to service the monastery and its hinterland.

Clonmacnoise has long been considered as being on the Esker Riada, the traditional primary east–west route across the midlands. This route would have made use of the dryland esker which rises above the surrounding raised bogs. The location of the Coolumber road, and its possible association with the bridge at Clonmacnoise, would make it a logical progression along this route and allow access to the dryland areas to the north-west of Coolumber Bog. The Bloomhill road does not follow the line of the esker but was constructed to the north of it. The linking of Bloomhill island by a series of gravel roads could not be considered part of the most logical, direct route to Clonmacnoise from the east or north-east. In fact, it appears to avoid both of these.

The amount of dryland around Clonmacnoise is relatively scarce and is generally confined to the esker ridges, parts of which are particularly steep. A large expanse of dryland, such as that at Bloomhill, may have been an important asset to the broader community which lived in the area of Clonmacnoise. As McDermott (1995, 66) suggests, the gravel road at Bloomhill may have been part of a wider network. This would have allowed access to the island itself and formed part of a wider infrastructure in the area of a large monastery such as Clonmacnoise.

It is also possible that some parts of the eskers may not have been suitable as communication routes, and the construction of gravel roads through the bogs may have been seen as a viable alternative. Whatever the reason, extensive gravel roads were constructed in the bogs around Clonmacnoise during the time the monastic centre was in existence. Some of the undated wooden toghers found in the surrounding bogs could also have formed part of a wider network of routes. However, the scale of bogland destruction in the area means that it is not possible to estimate the extent of any communication network at the time Clonmacnoise existed as a large monastic centre.

The occurrence of one or more gravel roads linking a relatively large dryland area, such as those found at Bloomhill, was also seen at Lemanaghan, Co. Offaly, another bog island to the east of Bloomhill which contains a monastic centre. Here the IAWU investigated a gravel road, similar to the Bloomhill road, which joins the island with the dryland to the east. This bog road is in line with an ancient 'togher' which leads eastwards from the monastery at the centre of Lemanaghan island, and it may be a continuation of this road. As with Bloomhill, the modern road which links the island with the dryland to the west is also said to have been constructed on the line of an older gravel road. The extent of archaeological remains in this area is particularly large, and the network of roads reflected in the Bloomhill evidence is more evident at Lemanaghan. In any event, the situation at Bloomhill is not unique, and the evidence from Lemanaghan suggests a more widespread use of gravel roads to link bog islands with the surrounding dryland.

References

Breen, T.C. 1988 Excavation of a roadway at Bloomhill Bog, Co. Offaly. *Proceedings of the Royal Irish Academy* **88C**, 321–39.

IAWU 1993 Excavations at Clonfinlough, Co. Offaly. *Irish Archaeological Wetland Unit Transactions* **2**. Crannóg, Dublin.

IAWU 1995 Blackwater Survey (Blackwater maps, townland list & catalogue). *Irish Archaeological Wetland Unit Transactions* **4**, 67–139. Crannóg, Dublin.

McDermott, C. 1995 A paved way in Bloomhill Bog in counties Westmeath and Offaly. *Irish Archaeological Wetland Unit Transactions* **4**, 59–66. Crannóg, Dublin.

Moloney, A. 1995 Blackwater Survey (introduction & survey results). *Irish Archaeological Wetland Unit Transactions* **4**, 1–6, 17–37. Crannóg, Dublin.

Moore, F. 1996 Ireland's oldest bridge at Clonmacnoise. *Archaeology Ireland* **10** (4), 24–7.

Raftery, B., Jennings, D. and Moloney, A. 1995 Annaghcorrib 1, Garryduff Bog, Co. Galway. *Irish Archaeological Wetland Unit Transactions* **4**, 39–53. Crannóg, Dublin.

3. THE LANDS OF ST CIARÁN

Annette Kehnel

Introduction

Clonmacnoise was certainly one of the greatest churches in medieval Ireland prior to the church reform of the twelfth century. One is used to thinking about Irish churches in terms of monasteries or monastic centres, implying that a main characteristic was that they were communities of religious men (and in some cases women), pious monks who lived together, spending their time in prayer, singing psalms and illustrating beautiful gospel-books. More recently, however, historians have put increasing emphasis on the fact that the Irish church was not, after all, organised very differently from the churches in the rest of Christian Europe.[1] As a result monasticism is dismissed as the most important feature of Irish church organisation. Using evidence from eighth-century canon law, one could, for example, show that the Irish bishops had in fact more rights and a higher position than was previously imagined. As the head of a church the bishop had jurisdictional power in spiritual affairs, i.e. like his colleagues in the Continental church he would appoint priests, perform ordinations, carry out visitations, consecrate the baptismal chrism and in general ensure the orderly maintenance of the church's ministry.[2] Correspondingly the abbot of an Irish church was not, as the title seems to imply, merely the head or father of a religious community. In fact the Irish annals most often refer to him as *princeps, airchinnech* or *comarba*. As is apparent from eighth-century canon law, this title was applied to the lay ruler of a church, who seems to have been the administrator of the temporalities. This means he not only presided over a community of monks but also had authority over the ecclesiastical tenants who lived in and around the settlement. We must also assume that, as the one in charge of the church's possessions, he was ultimately responsible for the collection of the rent from the lay people who lived and worked on the ecclesiastical lands.[3] Moreover, each of the great Irish churches had a number of dependencies, smaller churches under the pastoral jurisdiction of its bishop. It seems that this meant, in the first place, that the mother-church supplied a priest and that its bishop was, as in his own church, responsible for the due performance of the ministry. There was, of course, a financial side to this relationship—alms, fees for baptism and burial, as well as regular tithes, payable to the mother-church—which again would be administered by the abbot or *princeps*. Thus he had authority not only over the ecclesiastical tenants living near his own church but also over the people and lands belonging to the various churches in his *paruchia*. The *princeps* of a church would thus have had power over a large ecclesiastical estate ultimately dependent on rights of property, which has led scholars to talk about Irish churches in terms of ecclesiastical lordships, in which the powers of the *princeps* parallel those of a secular lord over a *tuath*.[4]

Hagiographical sources

With this background in mind, we might ask ourselves how much we know about the actual extent of such a medieval Irish ecclesiastical estate. In the present paper an attempt will be made to address this question in the case of Clonmacnoise. Hagiographical writings constitute a most valuable source in this regard. According to the current patterns of interpretation, hagiographical references to two churches or, most frequently, their founders, be they friendly or hostile, can in most cases be interpreted as statements concerning the relationship between the respective churches at the time the story was written down or subsequently revised.[5] Thus the cordial friendship which Ciarán is said to have cherished with Finnian, the founder saint of Clonard, would be a reflection of the close ties which

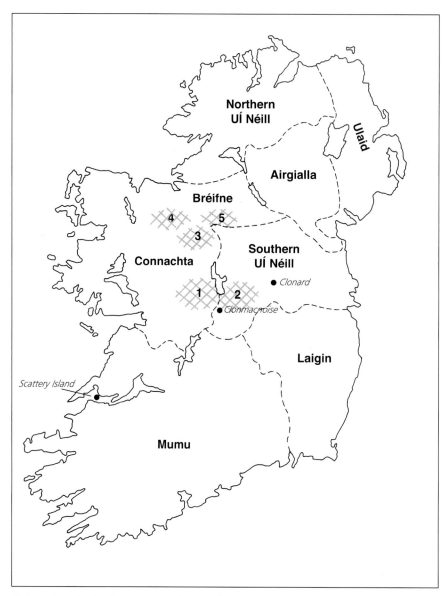

Ill. 1—Map of Ireland c. AD 800, showing the main political divisions. Hatched areas: 1=Uí Maine, 2=Ua Máelsechlainn kings of Mide, 3=Ua Conchobair kings of Connacht, 4=Mac Diarmada, 5= Uí Ruairc of Bréifne.

existed between the two churches in the tenth and early eleventh centuries, when Clonard and Clonmacnoise were often ruled by one abbot.[6] Another example here would be the hagiographer's portrayal of the relationship between St Ciarán and St Senán, the founder saint of Inis Cathaig on Scattery Island. We are told in the Life of St Ciarán that the two were very close friends. Once, on his way to Scattery Island, Ciarán is said to have met a poor man to whom he gave his cloak. Senán, foreseeing Ciarán's arrival and his nakedness, prepared a little surprise for his saintly friend, hiding a new cloak for Ciarán under his armpit, and giving it to him as a welcoming present. The meeting ended with the two saints celebrating Mass together, sharing holy communion and making a mutual agreement of perpetual friendship (*fraternitas*) between themselves and their successors.[7] Again, such a story would suggest a union between Clonmacnoise and St Senán's church on Scattery Island, which, situated in the estuary of the Shannon, was a central point for foreign trade in medieval Ireland, and therefore would have been a very useful ally to have from an economic point of view.[8]

According to the pattern of interpretation outlined above, medieval Irish hagiography testifies to links between Clonmacnoise and a large number of churches, including Inishkeen in County Monaghan in the east of Ireland, Devenish in County Fermanagh in the north, as well as churches in the north-western parts of Connacht, in County Sligo, and those in the north of Munster, like Roscrea or Inis Cathaig. St Ciarán's friends were all scattered within this large territory, constituting ecclesiastical units under the pastoral jurisdiction of the bishop and under the temporal rule of the *princeps* of Clonmacnoise. These churches acknowledged St Ciarán and his successors as their ecclesiastical overlords.

The 'Registry of Clonmacnoise'

So far we have outlined the sphere of influence of Clonmacnoise according to the evidence contained in hagiographical sources. It would, of course, be nice to have a genuine Clonmacnoise record of its possessions and holdings. In Armagh, for example, the contemporary historiographers brought forward a detailed list of the churches founded by St Patrick, implying that they should all be under the authority of St Patrick's church in Armagh.[9] For Clonmacnoise, unfortunately, nothing comparable to the *collectanea* of Tírechán or the work of Muirchú exists. There is, however, a hint pointing to the existence of a register of the church of Clonmacnoise, dating from the early seventeenth century. Around the year 1622 a survey of the diocese of Clonmacnoise, then united with Meath, was taken.[10] In the report the surveyors state that there existed a register of the lands belonging to Clonmacnoise, which, we are told, unfortunately got lost. However, it seems very plausible that someone translated this document into English on that occasion, and perhaps this is identical with the early seventeenth-century English text known as the 'Registry of Clonmacnoise', preserved amongst the manuscripts of James Ware, now lodged in the British Library (BL MSS Add. 4796, 36–43). It was edited by John O'Donovan in 1856.[11] The scribe tells us that he translated into easy English an earlier document which was drawn out of the 'auncient life of St. Kyran and the Red booke'.[12] He presents us with a list of lands and churches claimed to have been in the possession of the bishop of Clonmacnoise. Internal evidence seems to confirm his statement that he actually copied the 'Registry' from an earlier source, which ultimately might have depended on an original pre-reform account of the churches held by Clonmacnoise.[13]

This assumption tends to be confirmed by a careful reading of the 'Registry' alongside the political history of the church of St Ciarán in the pre-reform period, as it can be reconstructed from the medieval annals and contemporary hagiographical writings. Amongst the secular patrons of Clonmacnoise appear the kings of Mide of the Southern Uí Néill as well as the kings of Connacht and its various subkingdoms like Uí Maine or Bréifne. Precisely those people turn up in the 'Registry' as the benefactors of Clonmacnoise who are said to have endowed the church of Ciarán with lands and churches within their territory. Thus we find mention of the Ua Conchobair kings of Connacht, the Ua Máelsechlainn kings of Mide, the Ua Ruairc lords of Bréifne and the Ua Ceallaigh lords of Uí Maine. Also we are told that in return for their generosity they received the right to be buried in St Ciarán's graveyard, an important inducement, since by tradition no-one who was buried there would see damnation at the Day of Judgment.[14]

A number of the lands claimed as Clonmacnoise holdings in the 'Registry' can in fact be confirmed by evidence from genuine medieval sources. Let us take a few examples. The first dates from the early period, when the kings of Connacht appear as the most prominent secular lords active in Clonmacnoise. For a large proportion of the abbots of Clonmacnoise between the seventh and the ninth centuries a Connacht origin is attested.[15] From the contemporary annals we learn that between 744 and 814 St Ciarán's law was repeatedly proclaimed throughout Connacht.[16] As Kathleen Hughes has pointed out, the enactment of a saint's law, often associated with the carrying around of his relics, was an act by which ecclesiastical jurisdiction was exercised. It went hand in hand with the collection of the ecclesiastical fees and tithes.[17] Moreover, it generally presupposed the support of the secular rulers in the area, who in Connacht at the time were the kings of the up-and-coming Uí Briúin dynasty.[18] All in all, there seem to be good historical grounds on which to base the 'Registry's' claim that Clonmacnoise had authority over churches and lands in Connacht. In some cases we can even verify individual grants by comparing the place-names listed in the 'Registry' with what we learn from contemporary medieval sources. Amongst the donations given to Clonmacnoise by the Ua Conchobair kings of Connacht the document names, for example, certain lands in 'Tamhnagh'.[19] This claim seems to find confirmation in an incidental hint by Tírechán, the seventh-century biographer of St Patrick, who at one stage complains about the fact that Clonmacnoise got hold of many churches in Connacht which rightly should belong to Armagh, and mentions three churches by name. One of them is 'Tamnuch', which appears to be the modern parish of Tawnagh in County Sligo, north of Lough Arrow.[20] It seems highly plausible that both Tírechán and the 'Registry' refer to one and the same place. A similar reconstruction is possible in the case of 'Acha Obhair', mentioned in the 'Registry' as one of St Ciarán's churches in the very north of the territory of the Uí Maine. It appears that this was the name of a townland in the parish of Fuerty, now in County Roscommon.[21] Again an important hint is given by Tírechán, who testifies to links between Clonmacnoise and Fuerty by asserting that this was a church founded by Patrick in Uí Maine for a deacon named Justus, who is said to have, in his very old age, baptised the infant Ciarán.[22]

By the early tenth century the kings of Connacht had lost their influence at Clonmacnoise to the rising dynasties of the Southern Uí Néill from Mide. The latter first appear as generous benefactors of St Ciarán's church in the person of Flann Sinna, king of Tara, of the Clann Cholmáin between 887 and 916. He, together with the then abbot of Clonmacnoise, built a great stone church in the settlement, which later became known as the 'cathedral'.[23] It seems that the ascent to power of the kings of the Southern Uí Néill gave rise to a number of hagiographical tales linking the dynasty with Clonmacnoise from the very day of its foundation. Thus we are told that Diarmait mac Cerbaill, the ultimate ancestor of the Southern Uí Néill, assisted St Ciarán in erecting the first post for his church. The saint in return helped Diarmait to achieve the kingship of Tara. As a reward, the new king is said to have acknowledged St Ciarán's ecclesiastical authority throughout his realm and to have bestowed a hundred churches within his kingdom on the church of St Ciarán.[24] Despite the fact that none of these churches is listed by name, the tenth-century hagiographer testifies to the fact that Clonmacnoise held, or at least claimed, a number of churches in the medieval kingdom of Mide.

The annals provide similar evidence, this time regarding a particular Clonmacnoise dependency in Mide, namely 'Liathmanchain', now Lemanaghan in County Offaly, which is also listed amongst the lands of Clonmacnoise in the 'Registry'.[25] According to a gloss in the *Annals of Tigernach*, the lands there belonged to Clonmacnoise as early as the seventh century, when they were given to the community by King Diarmait, son of Aed Sláine, the founder of the Síl nÁedo Sláine, who were another royal branch of the Southern Uí Néill. The annalist tells us that the king made the donation as a reward for the community's support in the battle of Carn Conaill, which he fought and won against the king of Connacht in 649.[26] Since one of this king's descendants was king of Tara in the mid-tenth century, we might assume that this story dates from around that time, and that a privilege regarding Lemanaghan was granted to Clonmacnoise sometime during his reign.[27]

As a third and, for the present purpose, last example concerning the identification of former church lands mentioned in the 'Registry', we might choose a number of Clonmacnoise's holdings in the parishes of Kilcleagh and Ballyloughloe, now in County Westmeath, north-east of Clonmacnoise.[28] In this area was situated a church called Íseal Chiaráin, where, according to hagiographical tradition, two brothers of Ciarán used to live and with whom he stayed for some time before founding Clonmacnoise.[29] As is apparent from the annals, Íseal Chiaráin was a daughter-church of Clonmacnoise and rendered services and taxes to the princeps in Clonmacnoise down to the late eleventh century, when it eventually became independent.[30] It seems very plausible that the lands in Kilcleagh and Ballyloughloe, mentioned as St Ciarán's lands in the 'Registry', originally belonged to Clonmacnoise by right of property, resulting from the jurisdictional authority which the bishop exercised in the Clonmacnoise dependency of Íseal Chiaráin.

Since many of the lands claimed in the 'Registry' can be confirmed through such or comparable evidence, we might assume that the document represents—in a severely distorted form, of course—an original register kept in Clonmacnoise prior to the twelfth-century church reform. It might therefore serve as a genuine source for the reconstruction of the extent of the lands which once belonged to Clonmacnoise. They included a large proportion of the territory now represented by the counties of Offaly and Westmeath. Extensive holdings in Connacht are mentioned, a large proportion of which were situated in the area immediately west of Clonmacnoise, in the parishes of Moore and Creagh (the south of modern County Roscommon) and in east County Galway. Further lands are spread in what is now north County Roscommon, near Tulsk, and in south County Sligo, around Lough Gara and Lough Arrow. Finally, we find mention of six churches in Bréifne, which can be roughly located in what is now south County Leitrim.[31] The list of churches and lands belonging to Clonmacnoise as preserved in the 'Registry' shows an unmistakable bias towards lands in the extended neighbourhood of St Ciarán's church, mainly spread in Connacht and Mide. A comparison with the hagiographical evidence, discussed above, suggests that Clonmacnoise held further lands, as far north as Devenish, as far east as the Louth–Monaghan border and also in the north of Munster. Possibly some parts of the original Clonmacnoise register got lost, or were omitted in the course of its several late medieval redactions, but enough evidence survives—in the saint's lives, in the annals, and in the so-called 'Registry'—to show that the lands of St Ciarán extended far beyond the bounds of Clonmacnoise itself.

References

Bieler, L. (ed.) 1979 *The Patrician texts in the Book of Armagh*. Dublin.

Byrne, F.J. 1973 *Irish kings and high-kings*. London.

Cox, L. 1969 Íseal Chiaráin, the low place of St. Ciarán, where was it situated? *Journal of the Old Athlone Society* **1** (1), 6–14.

Doherty, C. 1987 The Irish hagiographer: resources, aims, results. In T. Dunne (ed.), *The writer as witness: literature as historical evidence*, 10–22. Historical Studies XVI. Cork University Press.

Elrington, C. (ed.) 1864 A Certificate of the State and Revennewes of the Bishoppricke of Meath and Clonemackenosh. In C. Elrington (ed.), *The whole works of the most Rev. James Ussher*, vol. 1, appendix 5, liii–ciiv. London.

Etchingham, C. 1992 Aspects of early Irish ecclesiastical organisation (2 vols). Unpublished Ph.D. thesis, Trinity College Dublin.

Etchingham, C. 1994 Bishops in the early Irish church: a re-assessment. *Studia Hibernica* No. 28, 35–62.

Heist, W. (ed.) 1965 *Vitae sanctorum Hiberniae*. Subsidia Hagiographica 28. Brussels.

Herbert, M. 1988 *Iona, Kells and Derry*. Oxford.

Hughes, K. 1987 The church and the world in Early Christian Ireland. In K. Hughes, *Church and society in Ireland A.D. 400–1200*, 99–116. London.

Kehnel, A. 1994 St. Ciarán's church and his lands. A study of the history and development of Clonmacnois. Unpublished Ph.D. thesis, Trinity College Dublin.

Kehnel, A. 1997 *Clonmacnoise—The church and lands of St Ciarán*. Münster.

Macalister, R.A.S. 1921 *Latin and Irish Lives of Ciaran*. London.

McCone, K. 1984 An introduction to early Irish saints' Lives. *Maynooth Review* **11**, 26–59.

Manning, C. 1994 *Clonmacnoise*. Dublin.

Nicholls, K.W. 1972 Some Patrician sites of eastern Connacht. *Dinnseanchas* **5**, 114–18.

O'Donovan, J. (ed.) 1856–7 The Registry of Clonmacnoise; with notes and introductory remarks. *Journal of the Royal Society of Antiquaries of Ireland* **4**, 444–60.

Plummer, C. (ed.) 1910 *Vitae sanctorum Hiberniae* (2 vols). Oxford.

Ryan, J. 1940 The abbatial succession at Clonmacnois. In J. Ryan (ed.), *Féil-scríbhinn Eóin Mhic Néill. Essays and studies presented to Professor Eoin MacNeill*, 490–507. Dublin.

Sharpe, R. 1984 Some problems concerning the organization of the church in early medieval Ireland. *Peritia* **3**, 230–70.

Simington, R. (ed.) 1949 *Books of Survey and Distribution, vol. I, Roscommon*. Dublin.

Stokes, W. (ed.) 1890 *Lives of the saints from the Book of Lismore*. Oxford.

Notes

1. Sharpe 1984, 230–47, for literature on the traditionalist 'monastic' approach; Etchingham 1992.
2. Sharpe 1984, 263; Etchingham 1994.
3. Sharpe 1984, 258, 263–5.
4. *Ibid.*, 264.
5. McCone 1984, 56; Doherty 1987, 11.
6. Plummer 1910, I, 205–6, §§15–17; Macalister 1921, 173–4, §§ 4–6; Heist 1965, 80–1, §§12–13; Stokes 1890, 122–7. The abbots who ruled both in Clonard and Clonmacnoise were Colmán, son of Ailill, d. 926 (*AU*); Céilechair, son of Robartach, d. 954 (*AU*); Flaithbertach, son of Domnall, d. 1014 (*AU*).
7. Stokes 1890, 128; Plummer 1910, I, 208–9; Macalister 1921, 177, §12.
8. Byrne 1973, 170.
9. Bieler 1979.
10. The bishop of Clonmacnoise and Meath at the time was James Ussher; Elrington 1864, lix.
11. O'Donovan 1856–7 (hereafter referred to as *Registry*).
12. *Registry*, 460.
13. For more details here see Kehnel 1994, 166–80; see also Kehnel 1997.
14. Stokes 1890, 127, ll 4261–2.
15. Compare Ryan 1940.
16. *AU* 744.9, *AI* 775, *AU* 788.9, *AU* 814.11.
17. Hughes 1987, 103.
18. Byrne 1973, 248–53.
19. *Registry*, 451.
20. Bieler 1979, 142–3, §25.2. For the identification of the place see Nicholls 1972, 114, n. 5.
21. *Registry*, 455; Simington 1949, 128.
22. According to Tírechán; see Bieler 1979, 128, §7.2; 146–7, §28.1–3.
23. *CS* 908 (*recte* 909); *AFM* 904; *AClon* 901, p. 144; see Manning 1994, 23–4, and this vol.

24. Stokes 1890, 130–1, ll 4379–98.
25. *Registry*, 449.
26. *AT* (649); the original report about the battle is given in Latin, the gloss is added in Middle Irish; compare also *CS* 646, *AClon* 642, p.104, *AU* 649.2.
27. This was Congalach, son of Máel Mithig, who held the kingship between 950 and 956; see Byrne 1973, 87, 281–2; compare also Herbert 1988, 158, 170.
28. *Registry,* 449, nn 4 and 5; 450, n. 12; 450, n. 17.
29. Stokes 1890, 119, l. 3998; 129, ll 4327–43. For the identification of the location of Íseal Chiaráin see Cox 1969.
30. In 1093 the head of Íseal Chiaráin bought freedom from taxation from the king of Mide and the abbot of Clonmacnoise; see *CS* 1089 (*recte* 1093), *AClon* 1087, p. 184.
31. A number of grants in Munster are also included in the Registry, but these appear to have been late medieval insertions.

Schoolchildren on a visit to Clonmacnoise, 1870–1914 (Lawrence Collection, NLI).

4. EARLY PHOTOGRAPHS OF CLONMACNOISE

John Scarry

Ill. 1—The Cross of the Scriptures, 1857 (courtesy of Dúchas, The Heritage Service).

The post-1850s period saw a rapid expansion in the use of photography in the Irish countryside. Although a number of photographic studios had been established a decade earlier, their main business was recording the family portrait. Most of these studios used a silver plate process, the daguerreotype, named after its French inventor, Louis Daguerre. This consisted of a positive image formed by mercury vapour on a polished coating of silver on a copper plate. An alternative process was the calotype paper negative system first demonstrated by William Fox Talbot in England in 1839. The basic process employed good-quality paper brushed over with a solution of silver iodide and potassium iodide. After a second coating, the paper could be exposed in the camera either wet or after drying, exposure being around five minutes at ƒ8 in bright sunlight. The calotype had an advantage over the daguerreotype in that multiple copies could be made from the negative, but because of patent restrictions it was mainly used as a hobby by relatively wealthy people.

By 1860 the daguerreotypes and calotypes were being replaced by the superior-quality collodion wet plate glass negative. This process was widely used despite the fact that photographers had to carry darkroom equipment and chemicals around with them on location. It is from this process that the earliest known photographs of Clonmacnoise come. Illustration 1, dated 1857, shows the Cross of the Scriptures leaning at an angle to the north, in front of the west door of the cathedral. It also shows the cathedral before conservation work.

These early photographs are particularly informative regarding the state of the buildings and crosses in the second half of the nineteenth century. A number of photographs in a collection known as the Stereo Collection (Lawrence) in the National Library of Ireland illustrate this point. (Stereo plates are two almost-identical images on one negative. When they are viewed through a stereoscope they give a three-dimensional effect.) Illustration 2, dating to the mid-1860s, shows the South Cross from the south-east with O'Rourke's round tower in the background. The head of the Cross of the Scriptures can be seen in front of the door of the tower, and the photograph shows that both crosses were leaning at that time. Illustration 3 shows the Cross of the Scriptures from the south-west, with the tower of Temple Finghin in the background and the north-west corner of the cathedral on the right. This photograph was taken before the cap of the tower was conserved in 1868 (see Ill. 16). Illustration 4 shows the South Cross from the south-west, with Temple Dowling and the sacristy of the cathedral in the background. One gets a good view of the second storey of the sacristy with its fine octagonal chimney. The sacristy was added in the fifteenth century as residential accommodation. The original access to this floor was through a high-level doorway in the west wall where it joined the cathedral. This was subsequently blocked up. This photograph also shows a ragged hole in the west wall of the sacristy where the modern access to the first floor was located. Illustration 5, from a print in the Royal Irish Academy, is a close-up view of the South Cross and probably dates from the 1860s too.

Also dating from the same period are a number of photographs from the Dunraven Collection. Edwin, the third earl of Dunraven, travelled extensively throughout Ireland during the summer months of 1866–9. He visited many Early Christian sites for his discourse on early Irish architecture, which was published, following his death, in two volumes, in 1875 and 1877 respectively. Accompanying the earl on his trips were Dr William Stokes, his daughter Margaret and Mr William Mercer of Rathmines, Dublin. William Mercer was a little-known photographer who produced work of the highest quality, as can be seen from Illustrations 6–10.

Illustration 6 is an unusual perspective of O'Rourke's Tower and the Cross of the Scriptures, as it appears to give the impression that the cross is much closer to the round tower than it is in reality. Illustration 7 is a view of St Finghin's church and tower from the south-east prior to the reconstruction work undertaken by James Graves and the Kilkenny Archaeological Society in 1868 (Graves 1868, 141–2; 1869, 214). Illustration 8 is an internal view of Temple Finghin from the west; Illustration 9 is also an internal view but of the east window of Temple Rí, while Illustration 10 shows the chancel arch of the Nuns' Church with the east wall before reconstruction. Again, because we know that Graves and the Kilkenny Archaeological Society repaired this building in 1865, the photograph shows the structure before the repair works were carried out (Graves 1864–5).

The photographs reproduced here from vol. 2 of Dunraven's *Notes on Irish architecture* are copies of the original Woodbury-type prints. It is a pity that this printing process ceased to be used, as the prints were significantly more permanent than the photographic prints of the time and are without the screen effect of other printing methods.

The Commissioners of Public Works commissioned the firm of Ward & Company of Cork to take some photographs of sites in their care in the period 1865–70. Illustration 11, showing a wide-angle view of the monastic site, is thought to have been taken by this company, while Illustration 12 shows the Nuns' Church following the restoration by the Kilkenny Archaeological Society (cf. Ill. 10). The plaque outlining the work undertaken by the Society can be seen in Illustration 13 on the internal west wall of the church. It reads:

> In May A.D. 1865/ by the aid of subscriptions/ and under the inspection
> of/ the Rev. James Graves/Hon. Sec. Kilkenny South East of/ Ireland
> Archaeological Society/ the fallen choir arch and door/ of this church
> originally built/A.D. 1167 were re-erected.

Illustration 14 is a view of the internal south wall of the cathedral, while Illustration 15 is a wide-angle view of Temple Rí and Temple Hurpan from the south-east. Illustration 16 shows St Finghin's church with the cap of its round tower restored (cf. Ill. 7) and, as we know this was done in 1868, the photograph post-dates this work.

The late 1870s saw the introduction of dry-coated glass plates, a process which remained in general use for many decades even after the introduction of cellulose roll film. A major collection of photographs in the National Library of Ireland, known as the Lawrence Collection, uses this process and dates from the period 1870–1914. It comprises the work of several photographers, the most notable of whom was Robert French, who took most of the location photographs. The Lawrence Company produced commercial work which would often be used to make postcards for sale to the public. As Clonmacnoise was rightly regarded as one of the major historic sites, along with Glendalough and the Rock of Cashel, it was frequently visited by early photographers. Illustration 17 is a general shot of the monastic site from the south, while Illustration 18 is a view of the site from the west with the Cross of the Scriptures, the South Cross, the cathedral and Temple Dowling. Illustration 19 and the frontispiece to this paper, are wonderfully atmospheric and nostalgic views of Clonmacnoise in an era when one could not imagine the busloads of tourists which now descend on the site from all over the world.

Another well-known photographer, Robert J. Welch of Belfast, visited the site in July 1914 and took a series of photographs of the more popular views. His photograph of the fifteenth-century north door of the cathedral (Ill. 20) is especially interesting as it would appear to be the earliest photograph of that feature and shows the plastered surface surrounding the figures of saints Patrick, Francis and Dominic. It also illustrates the foundations of the door and the eroded ground surface at the base of the doorway at that time.

Prior to major conservation works being undertaken by the Office of Public Works in the late 1950s, their staff photographer, James Bambury, took a number of views in 1956. Illustration 21 is another atmospheric view of the site from the south-east, with a dead tree and sheep grazing among the tombstones. Illustration 22 shows the beginning of the tidying up in the old burial-ground and the original oratory which was built in the 1930s and subsequently taken down in 1968.

In conclusion, it is worth mentioning that Clonmacnoise has long been a place visited by the pilgrim, the tourist or the interested passer-by. It was also an important site for visits from various field clubs and photographic societies which had sprung up around the country in the latter half of the nineteenth century. Many of the photographs taken by these groups and individuals during the late nineteenth and early twentieth centuries are probably lost, but many others may still survive in private ownership. These photographs could be of enormous help in elucidating the architectural and archaeological history not only of Clonmacnoise but also of other Irish monuments. It would be of great benefit to future historical research if a comprehensive inventory of nineteenth-century photographs of field monuments could be compiled. At present the importance of photographic archives, such as those maintained by the Heritage Service, the Irish Architectural Archive and the National Library of Ireland, cannot be overstated as they are an essential visual national resource, and if the reader of this paper knows of old photographs of the site it would be greatly appreciated if the owner(s) would get in touch with *Dúchas,* The Heritage Service Photographic Archive.

Acknowledgements

I would like to thank Heather King and Con Manning for their observations and remarks on the content of the photographs, Edward Chandler for information on William Mercer, the Trustees of the National Library of Ireland for permission to reproduce Illustrations 2–4 and 17–19, the Trustees of the National Museums and Galleries of Northern Ireland for Illustration 20, and the Royal Irish Academy for Illustration 5. Illustrations 6–10 are taken from Dunraven's *Notes on Irish architecture,* vol. 2, and the remaining photographs are from the Heritage Service Photographic Archive.

References

Graves, J. 1864–5 Proceedings. *Journal of the Royal Society of Antiquaries of Ireland* **8**, 367–70.
Graves, J. 1868–9 Proceedings. *Journal of the Royal Society of Antiquaries of Ireland* **10**, 139–63, 209–43.

Photographic sources for Clonmacnoise

Dúchas, The Heritage Service Photographic Archive
Clonmacnoise print files include over 3000 negatives from 1860 to the present day.
1. General views and details
2. The Cross of the Scriptures
3. The Nuns' Church and the castle
4. The Early Christian slabs
5. Excavation

The National Library of Ireland
Lawrence Collection:
Royal   2941–5, 2947, 5149, 5269–76
Imperial   2254–5, 3519–20, 3522–3, 3606
Cabinet   23–4, 2295–2300, 3840, 5394–8, 6937–9, 6941, 6943
New Series   8776–7 Royal. 8780. Stereo Collection 526–8, 2884.
The Valentine Collection 61767–61968

The Ulster Museum, Belfast
Welch Collection; W30, Co. Offaly, Clonmacnoise
1. General view
2. Cathedral doorway
3. Teampull Finghin, chancel arch
4. Teampull Finghin and round tower
5. Round tower
6. Cross of the Scriptures and round tower

Dunraven: Notes on Irish architecture, *vol. 2 (London, 1877)*
Plate LXXXI: O'Rourke's Tower, facing p. 32
Plates LXXXIX & XC: St Finghin's Church, p. 46
Plates CXIII & CXIV: The Nuns' Church, p. 102
Plate CXV: East window of O'Melaghlin's Church, p. 106

Royal Irish Academy
Three photographic prints: one of the Cross of the Scriptures and two of the South Cross

Birr Castle Photographic Collection
Photographs of Clonmacnoise (uncatalogued)

Ill. 2—The South Cross from the south-east with O'Rourke's round tower in the background, mid-1860s (Stereo Collection, NLI).

Ill. 3—The Cross of the Scriptures, mid-1860s (Stereo Collection, NLI).

Ill. 4—The South Cross from the south-west, with Temple Dowling and the sacristy of the cathedral in the background, mid-1860s (Stereo Collection, NLI).

Ill. 5—West face of the South Cross (Royal Irish Academy).

Ill. 6—O'Rourke's Tower and the Cross of the Scriptures, 1866–9 (Dunraven Collection).

Ill. 7—St Finghin's church and tower from the south-east, 1866–9 (Dunraven Collection).

Ill. 8—Internal view of Temple Finghin from the west, 1866–9 (Dunraven Collection).

Ill. 9—Internal view of the east window of Temple Rí, 1866–9 (Dunraven Collection).

Ill. 10—The chancel arch of the Nuns' Church with the unreconstructed east wall, 1866–9 (Dunraven Collection).

Ill. 11—General view of the monastic site from the north, c. 1870 (Ward & Co., Cork).

Ill. 12—The Nuns' Church following restoration, c. 1870 (Ward & Co., Cork).

Ill. 13—The Nuns' Church from the east, c. 1870 (Ward & Co., Cork).

Ill. 14—The internal south wall of the cathedral, c. 1870 (Ward & Co., Cork).

Ill. 15—Temple Rí and Temple Dowling from the south-east, c. 1870 (Ward & Co., Cork).

Ill. 16—St Finghin's church, post-1867 (Ward & Co., Cork).

Ill. 17—The monastic site from the south, 1870–1914 (Lawrence Collection, NLI).

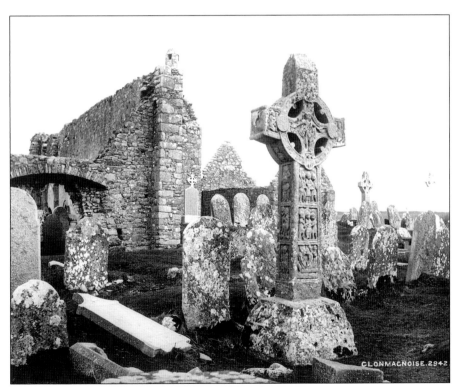

Ill. 18—The Cross of the Scriptures, the South Cross, the cathedral and Temple Dowling from the west, 1870–1914 (Lawrence Collection, NLI).

Ill. 19—Picnic at Clonmacnoise, 1870–1914 (Lawrence Collection, NLI).

Ill. 20—The fifteenth-century north door of the cathedral, 1914 (Robert J. Welch, Trustee of the National Museums and Galleries of Northern Ireland).

Ill. 21—General view of the site from the south-east, taken by James Bambury in 1956 (Dúchas, The Heritage Service).

Ill. 22—St Finghin's church and original oratory, taken by James Bambury in 1956 (Dúchas, The Heritage Service).

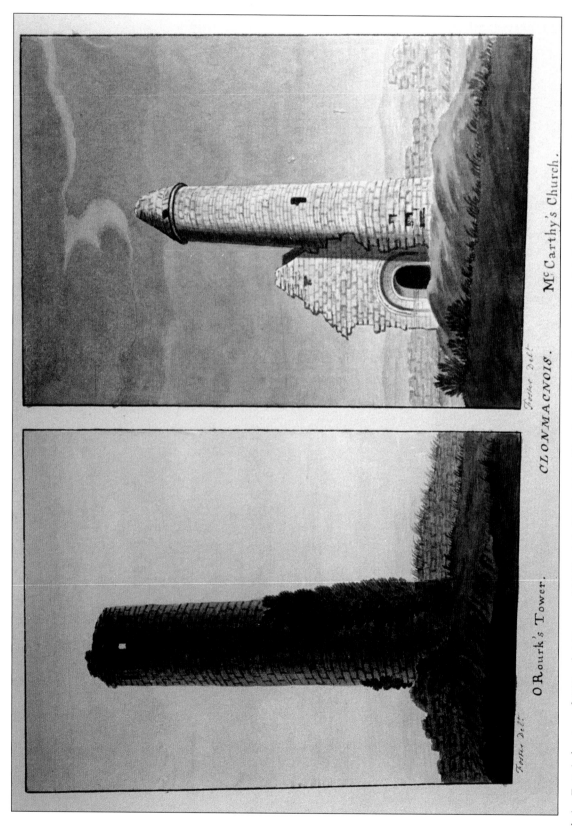

Ill. 1.—Foster's drawings of O'Rourke's Tower and McCarthy's (St Finghin's) Church as copied by Beranger. (Special Collections in the Library of University College Dublin.)

5. FOUR LATE EIGHTEENTH-CENTURY WATERCOLOUR DRAWINGS OF CLONMACNOISE ANTIQUITIES

Peter Harbison

In a recent article, Conleth Manning (1994) has placed us all in his debt by reproducing (and thereby making more generally available) the oldest published drawings of Clonmacnoise antiquities, namely the bird's-eye view in the second (1658) edition of *De Hibernia et antiquitatibus eius disquisitiones* by Sir James Ware (1594–1666), and the plan, views and details based on the sketches of J. Blaymires which appeared in Walter Harris's 1739 edition of Ware. The purpose of this note is to present four watercolours which show the state of some of the monuments about 40 years after Blaymires visited the site.

Although not signed by him, the watercolours almost certainly stem from the hand of Gabriel Beranger, an artist of French Huguenot origin who lived in Ireland from about 1751 until his death in 1817. Though soon forgotten thereafter, his revival was championed by Sir William Wilde, who published a series of articles about him (Wilde 1870–1; 1872–3; 1876–7) which were later reprinted together in a posthumous monographic *Memoir* (Wilde 1880), completed by Wilde's widow, Jane Francesca, better known under her poetic pseudonym 'Speranza'. On pages 7–8 of an appendix to this monograph, Wilde drew attention to the existence of a number of Beranger drawings in a 'Sketch-Book' which, in Wilde's day, was owned by the antiquarian J. Huband Smith, and which seems to have consisted of a considerable number of unbound sheets. Their contents, as listed by Wilde, correspond so closely to those of a Dublin private collection of Beranger drawings which remained intact until 1965 that the two were almost certainly identical. Probably some time in the first quarter of this century, the drawings had come into the possession of John Vickers McAlpine, who bequeathed them to his fourth daughter, Maud, who married a Mr Mossop. This information I was given by her daughter-in-law, Mrs Pauline Mossop, who kindly brought the collection to my attention in the first place and who placed at my disposal a copy of the inventory of the contents compiled by Maud Mossop before she offered the individual drawings for private sale sometime around the autumn of 1965. A considerable number of the sheets were acquired at the time by University College, Dublin, where they are now housed in the Special Collections of the College's Library, through the kindness of whose curator, Norma Jessop, I am enabled to publish here the two sheets bearing the Clonmacnoise material, with the inventory numbers Wat. 22–23.

It will be noted that Clonmacnoise does not feature in Wilde's appendix among the places illustrated by Beranger in the Huband Smith 'Sketch-Book'. The reason for this is that Wilde only listed those drawings which bore Beranger signatures and which were, in my view, based on earlier—but no longer traceable—sketches executed by Beranger himself. Yet Wilde also noted that the 'Sketch-Book' contained further 'drawings of considerable interest by Vallancey, Fisher, Burton-Conyngham, Grahame, Barrett and other well-known artists, of ancient castles and antiquarian monuments, not included in Beranger's set of illustrations'. Here, I consider, Wilde erred in attributing the drawings to those artists who are given as having *drawn* them; the uniform format, script and style of all the pictures in the 'Sketch-Book' would, rather, suggest that they were totally the work of Beranger, who, where he did not base himself on his own drawings, seems to have copied lost original sketches by other artists, whose names he carefully credited on the bottom left of the drawings. One of the artists whose work I believe Beranger copied in the Huband Smith 'Sketch-Book', but who was not specifically mentioned by Wilde, was someone

35

Ill. 2—Foster's drawings of Temple McDermot (the Cathedral) and Temple Doolin as copied by Beranger. (Special Collections in the Library of University College Dublin.)

named Foster. That Foster was the artist who originally drew the four Clonmacnoise watercolours illustrated here is faithfully recorded by Beranger, who wrote *Foster delt* (for *delineavit* = drew) beneath the bottom left-hand corner of each picture. Beranger was not the only one to copy Foster's original sketches, as an almost identical set of the Clonmacnoise pictures, painted ('*pinx*[*it*]') by the Rev. Joseph Turner in May 1799, are preserved on pages 39, 40, 45 and 49 of the Royal Irish Academy's manuscript 3.C.33—all marked 'Foster *delin.*' and clearly based on the same originals. In short, I believe that the watercolours reproduced here are copies by Beranger of lost originals drawn by Foster. It may be mentioned in parentheses here that page 46 of the same Academy manuscript bears a drawing of the Norman castle at Clonmacnoise entitled 'Remains of the Palace of Melaghlin', which is also based on a drawing by Foster. Neither Beranger nor Turner furnish us with either a Christian name or even an initial for Foster, but he can in all probability be equated with the John Foster named by Pasquin (1796?, 16) as having studied at Paris and who practised 'as a landscape painter in crayons and black chalk'. In W. G. Strickland's *Dictionary of Irish artists* (Dublin, 1913), 376, he is listed as John Foster, with a *floruit* between 1773 and 1780—a period which fits in very well with the date for these Clonmacnoise drawings suggested below.

But even if the originals on which the drawings were based were not by Beranger, we do know that Beranger visited Clonmacnoise himself. Proof of this is provided in a letter covering pages 103–6 of MS 1415 in the National Library of Ireland. The passages relevant to the site are reproduced here in an Appendix from my original publication of a quarter of a century ago (Harbison 1972–3), to which the late N. W. English kindly supplied the notes. At that time, I gave the likely recipient of the letter as Col. Charles Vallancey, but subsequent research has convinced me that it was almost certainly addressed to Col. William Burton—later Conyngham (see Trench 1985, 40). It was he who sent Beranger on a tour of Connacht and Ulster in the summer of 1779, during which he and his Italian artist friend Angelo Maria Bigari visited Clonmacnoise, presumably in order to augment pictorial material being collected by Burton for one or more volumes illustrating Irish antiquities intended for publication by the Hibernian Antiquarian Society (Love 1962), which was founded by Burton and others in 1779. As it transpired, not a single one of the volumes ever appeared, but some of the drawings which Burton had collected for the purpose were subsequently used by Edward Ledwich in Francis Grose's *Antiquities of Ireland,* which Ledwich edited after Grose's death in 1791. Though it can no longer be proven, it is quite likely that the Foster originals were among the portfolio of drawings which Burton was assembling around 1779 for the planned publication; there they would have been available for copying by Beranger and, even after Burton's death in 1796, also by Turner. If this supposition be correct, a date in—or not long before—1779 could be suggested for the execution of Foster's original Clonmacnoise sketches, and Beranger's copies are unlikely to be more than a year or two later.

After the background, now to the drawings themselves. They are on two separate sheets, each of which bears two pictures. One combines 'O'Rourk's Tower' and 'McCarthy's Church' (Ill. 1), and the other 'Temple McDermot' and 'Temple Doolin' (Ill. 2). O'Rourke's Tower, which still bears the name, is shown from the north-west, and differs little from its present appearance except, of course, for the ivy, absent for more than a century now, courtesy of the Board of Works. The stone walls, obviously later, abutting on to different sides of the tower show that the round tower was clearly at the boundary of the old churchyard where today it forms the extreme western tip.

It shares a sheet with 'McCarthy's Church', an old name for St Finghin's, the Romanesque church with inbuilt round tower on the northern rim of the churchyard. The gabled wall above the chancel arch was only marginally better preserved when Foster saw it, but his details of the arch itself would appear to be unreliable. The stones shown missing at the bottom of the tower have been replaced, and the hole at the base of the conical cap also seems to have been made good in the intervening centuries. Interestingly, the top of the conical roof is shown as missing. Blaymires showed it as complete in 1739, so that the pinnacle may have suffered slight damage in the 40 years before Foster drew it, and James Graves and the Kilkenny Archaeological Society repaired it in 1868 (see Scarry, this volume). From his standpoint, very similar to that of the camera which took the photograph reproduced by Macalister (1909, pl. XXVa), the artist shows a long, low, grassy mound which may have incorporated masonry from the nave of the church, including perhaps parts of the lowermost course of the south wall visible today. But the watercolour does bring home to us how much of the present nave is the result of reconstruction. Somewhat unexpected— and perhaps fanciful—is the angle of the wall seen running in a roughly north–south direction behind the church.

The second of the two sheets—Wat. 23 in the UCD Special Collections—has, on the left, an illustration of 'Temple McDermot', which is better known as the Cathedral. In it, the doorway can be seen to be better preserved than it is today. However, the scale of Blaymires's drawing (Manning 1994, 19) allows for more attention to valuable detail, including the leaf-decorated capitals and a surprisingly high-pointed Gothic arch, in envisaging the appearance of the doorway more than two centuries ago. The reason for the off-centre positioning of the doorway is explained by Conleth Manning in his contribution to this volume, namely that the south wall of the Cathedral was originally some feet further south, which would have made the doorway central in the west gable.

One of the more valuable aspects of this drawing is the view it provides of the interior of the east gable, most of which has since collapsed. As Conleth Manning pointed out to me, the top of a window embrasure, visible in the right-hand side of the gable, is that of a first-floor window of fifteenth-century date, which served the chamber above the vaulted east end of the Cathedral. This chamber had a door connecting it with the chamber above the sacristy (Manning, this volume). George Petrie's view from the east, engraved in the second volume of J. N. Brewer's *The beauties of Ireland* (London, 1826; see Manning, this vol., ill. 28), shows this window, and also indicates that the main east window had fifteenth-century switch-line tracery with a single mullion, like that still surviving in the south wall. The small rectangular feature visible through the doorway is difficult to interpret, but it might have been a wall niche.

Some other features of the drawing deserve notice. One is that the doorway, since the days of Blaymires, seems to have acquired an inner support on the south side going up above the level of the capitals, presumably in an attempt to prevent the collapse which was subsequently to take on more extensive proportions. Another concerns the window which let in light to the upper floor of the sacristy through its west wall. Its upper section no longer survives, but the drawing suggests that it was a pointed window with a hood-moulding in the late Gothic style. A third feature is the mound against the south wall of the Cathedral. This is the grassed-over and partly collapsed remains of an external platform and stairs in this angle which gave access to the first-floor doorway to the chamber above the sacristy (Manning, this volume). One final point concerns the broad (pilgrims'?) path that leads to the west door of the Cathedral. It comes in a broad sweep from the left— presumably to circumvent the Cross of the Scriptures, on the base of which the artist probably sat to make his drawing.

Sharing the sheet with the view of the Cathedral is the watercolour of Temple Doolin, which shows the church much as it is today, but with the addition of a large (secondary?) cross on top of the west gable, which is no longer present. The artist would appear to have taken some licence with the positioning of the—somewhat precariously leaning—South

Cross in front of the church, whereas today it (or, rather, its modern copy) can be seen to be to the south of the line of the south wall of the church. This picture is the only one to illustrate small upright headstones—showing how few burial monuments stood in the churchyard around 1779, before the following century and a half choked the place with them until the mid-1950s, when Percy LeClerc and the Office of Public Works got the much-appreciated approval of families with burial rights to lay most of the stones flat and flush with the ground.

The watercolours reproduced here, like others in Beranger's *oeuvre* (compare Harbison 1991; 1997; 1998), are not without their artistic merit. They are also interesting in showing us the state of some of the major Clonmacnoise monuments around the beginning of the last quarter of the eighteenth century, and they also help in filling out the period between Blaymires and Petrie. Each of the pictures is interesting in its own way, but probably the most valuable of them is that of the Cathedral, which sheds interesting light on features which have sadly disappeared in the intervening centuries.

Acknowledgements

I would like to express my gratitude to four ladies and three men who have provided valuable help in the course of preparing this article. Among the ladies, my thanks firstly to Norma Jessop, curator of Special Collections in the Library of University College, Dublin, for her, and the College's, permission to reproduce the watercolours which illustrate the article. Secondly, to Mrs Pauline L. Mossop of Terenure for providing information on the ownership of the 'Sketch-Book' after Huband Smith, when it belonged to her husband's forebears. Thirdly, to Siobhán O'Rafferty, librarian of the Royal Irish Academy, who assisted me in connection with the watercolours by the Rev. Joseph Turner in the Academy's collection, and last, but by no means least, Heather King for all her encouragement in inviting me to participate in the on-site seminar and to publish my findings here. The three men to whom I would like to express my thanks are Brian Lynch of Bord Fáilte, who took the photographs, Brendan O'Donoghue, Acting Director of the National Library, for his and his Trustees' permission to reproduce again extracts from Beranger's letter, and Conleth Manning, who read the typescript and made valuable additions and suggestions for its improvement.

References

Grose, F. 1791 *The antiquities of Ireland* (2 vols). London.

Harbison, P. 1972–3 Clonmacnois by Beranger, 1779 (with notes by N. W. English). *Journal of the Old Athlone Society* **1** (3), 195–6.

Harbison, P. 1991 *Beranger's views of Ireland*. Royal Irish Academy, Dublin.

Harbison, P. 1997 Beranger's copies of eighteenth-century views of Kilkenny. In J. Kirwan (ed.), *Kilkenny. Studies in honour of Margaret Phelan*, 98–103. The Kilkenny Archaeological Society.

Harbison, P. (ed.) 1998 *Gabriel Beranger; Drawings of the principal antique buildings of Ireland. National Library of Ireland MS 1958 TX*. Dublin.

Love, W.D. 1962 The Hibernian Antiquarian Society. *Studies* **51**, No. 203 (Autumn 1962), 419–31.

Macalister, R.A.S. 1909 *The memorial slabs of Clonmacnois, King's County: with an appendix on the materials for a history of the monastery*. Extra volume of the Royal Society of Antiquaries of Ireland for 1907–8. Dublin.

Manning, C. 1994 The earliest plans of Clonmacnoise. *Archaeology Ireland* **8** (1), 18–20.

Pasquin, A. 1796? *An authentic history of the professors of painting, sculpture & architecture, who have practised in Ireland*. London.

Trench, C.E.F. 1985 William Burton Conyngham (1733–1796). *Journal of the Royal Society of Antiquaries of Ireland* **115**, 40–63.

Wilde, W.R. 1870–1 Memoir of Gabriel Beranger, and his labours in the cause of Irish art, literature, and antiquities, from 1760 to 1780. *Journal of the Royal Society of Antiquaries of Ireland* **11**, 33–64, 121–52 and 236–60.

Wilde, W.R. 1872–3 Memoir of Gabriel Beranger, and his labours in the cause of Irish art, literature, and antiquities, from 1760 to 1780. *Journal of the Royal Society of Antiquaries of Ireland* **12**, 445–85.

Wilde, W.R. 1876–7 Memoir of Gabriel Beranger, and his labours in the cause of Irish art, literature, and antiquities, from 1760 to 1780. *Journal of the Royal Society of Antiquaries of Ireland* **14**, 111–56.

Wilde, W. R. 1880 *Memoir of Gabriel Beranger, and his labours in the cause of Irish art, literature, and antiquities, from 1760 to 1780.* Dublin.

APPENDIX
Extracts from a letter by Gabriel Beranger, describing a visit to Clonmacnoise in 1779

Originally published in Volume 1 (3) of *The Journal of the Old Athlone Society* for 1972–3, together with notes by the late N. W. English, which are reproduced here. The letter was written around the middle of August 1779, and was probably addressed to Col. William Burton. It is preserved as pages 103–6 of Manuscript 1415 of the National Library of Ireland, and reprinted here with its kind permission.

[ATHLONE][1]

Sir

We have been at Clonmacnois full of hopes of finding great antiquities, but were mistaken and found nothing equal to our Expectations, Except the Two round Towers, who undoubtedly are like those of their kind of unknown creation. They are Exedingly well built of hewn Stone but not of the highest Kind, one being 56 feet high including its Cap or Piramidal roof & the other without cap 62. the other Buildings aforded nothing Extraordinary above a Common Wall, an inscription, in the Largest upon the wall is as follows, in Roman characters on a Large flagg inlaid in the wall with a molding.

> Carolus Coghlanus, vicarius Generalis Cluanmacnose proprys impendys hanc Dirutam Eclesiam Restauravit Anno Dom 1647

and on another of the churches was the following English inscription on a Large flagg under a Coat of Arms in the front of the building over the Entrance

> M. Edmund Dowling of Clondalare who built this chappel to the Greater Glory of God & use of his posterity 1689

I believe that there was formerly some building or Other of antiquity, as the large church which they call The Cathedral, and which has the above Latin inscription, seems to be build of cut mountain Stone, the Corners of which Stones are worn away & Look roundish & filled up with morter, which makes me believe they were Old materials Employed to rebuilt this church, you shall be more able to determine on seeing the drawings. it was a tedious job, as Clonmacnois is 12 miles from this place by Land & 10 by water, Mr Kelly of Castle Kelly had given us Letters for Mr Moony[2] within 5 miles of Clonmacnois. but on our arrival he was abroad & the house So full of Comp:[ny] that his Lady was Sorry She could not Spare us a bed, She invited us at diner, which we declined & Sett out for Clonmacnois where we spend the whole day & came here to diner at 9. next day we sett of with day light by water ,,to Save our horse,, taking our dinner with us, & arrived there in three hours, we worked hard, & took various views & plans, I inquired for the Anchorites, but the people thereabouts did not hear of them, our recommendations here, was from Lady Ann Talbot to Mrs Wills, whose husband being abroad, She invited us to tea where we found 2 gentlemen, of whom & Some acquaintance I picked up, we Learn'd that those Seven Churches are not Looked upon as great antiques, but that the oldest & most curious ones are those of Glandalough, So that we are glad, that the accounts agree So well, We are here at an inn, where I shall make as little Stay as possible, & hope to go to morrow. for Mount Murray,[3] we are inking our drawings.

[What follows is an account of some financial affairs. The letter continues:]

The doors of the Seven Churches particularly of the Cathedrall are carved & Somewhat in the taste of the Abbey of Cong. the other, doors are round & plastered to make them even, the plaster is another Sign of modern work as in the old Buildings it is all destroyed by time, in Harris's translation of Ware, they are pretty well represented, also the Crosses which since that time are much wore, children throwing Stones at them & the figures blunted, & just the form seen the plan of D^{o} is pretty Correct, I have marked on it the buildings which have been destroyed since, & the one which is roofed & mended Serving for a Parish Church.

I hope you excuse the hurry of this Letter, as I am imployed in drawing, & want to finish to day to have done at the inn & go off to morrow

I have the Honour to be with respect

Sir Your most ob^t & most humble Servant

Gab^l Beranger

Bigary present his respects to you

P.S. Mr. Talbot got our Spring mended with Clips, which with the iron fork which suports it will bring us to Dublin he would not tell the Expences attending it, So it cost us nothing.

Notes

1. This letter was undoubtedly written from Athlone, internal evidence confirms, 'as Clonmacnois is 12 miles from this place by Land & 10 by water'. The letter does not appear in Wilde's 'Memoirs of Beranger'.
2. This refers to the Moony family (now Enraght-Moony), who still reside at The Doon.
3. Probably Mount Murray, near Bunbrusna, Co. Westmeath, still in occupation of the Murray family.

6. THE MONASTIC TOWN OF CLONMACNOISE

John Bradley

As annsin roclann Ciarán an cetcleath i Cluain

In recent years the appellation 'monastic town' has acquired a wide currency, replacing alternatives like 'proto-town' and 'pre-urban nucleus' in all except theoretical quarters. In large measure this is due to the work of Charles Doherty, whose 1985 paper was the first rigorous examination of the subject.[1] There are, however, several unsolved questions. Should seventh-century Kildare be described as a monastic town, for instance, because of the notices by Cogitosus, or should the term 'monastic town' be restricted to settlements after AD 800 (or indeed 900), when there is better documentation for the presence of markets and fairs, of streets and houses? How many monastic towns were there? Was every monastery a monastic town or were monastic towns scarce? Were there 'monastic villages' as distinct from 'monastic towns'? One of the difficulties in answering such questions is the absence of individual case studies which would facilitate comparisons and contrasts. This paper is a contribution to that process and it seeks to address the issues of the physical appearance, layout and extent of the monastic town at Clonmacnoise.

Historical background

The monastery of Clonmacnoise was established on what was effectively an island in the River Shannon, bounded directly by water on the north and surrounded elsewhere by an expanse of bog which stretched for miles in all directions. Despite its apparent isolation, the site was positioned close to the intersection of two major routeways, the River Shannon, running north/south, and the *eiscir riada*, a glacial ridge aligned east–west, which had formed a natural routeway across Ireland from prehistoric times. The founder of the monastery was St Ciarán, who died in, or about, 549.[2] According to the tradition recorded in the *Vitae Ciaráni*, the monastery was established for no more than six months when he died, and it has been suggested that Ciarán's death was caused by the Justinian plague, that great pestilence which devastated Constantinople and the eastern Mediterranean in 542/3 and by 545 had reached Ireland, where it flared up again in 549.[3] Death as a result of plague at least provides a simple explanation for Ciarán's comparatively early death (he is said to have been 33) as well as a context for his alleged dying words, in which he advised his fellow monks to seek out secluded places and to abandon his remains as one would 'the lifeless bones of a stag on the mountain'.[4] The account which attributes the foundation of the monastery to the joint efforts of Ciarán and the exiled Diarmait mac Cerbaill (high-king of Ireland from 544 to 564/5) is extremely doubtful and has all the appearance of a story which was concocted in the late ninth century to provide historical respectability to the patronage of Clonmacnoise by Diarmait's descendants, the Clann Cholmáin kings of Mide. Early documentation on Clonmacnoise is slight, but it was important enough as an ecclesiastical centre to merit consultation by Cummian, prior to the sending of his pastoral letter in 632/3, and by the close of the seventh century it had developed into one of the major midland monasteries.[5] Tírechán, writing *c.* 690, regarded Clonmacnoise as Armagh's major rival in the midlands and accused it of seizing churches, in the aftermath of 'the most recent plagues' (presumably those of 680–4), in the Sligo area which belonged by right to Armagh.[6] It was significant enough for Adomnán of Iona, writing *c.* 697, not only to notice Clonmacnoise but to mention it favourably. Indeed, it is Adomnán who supplies the sole documentary evidence that Clonmacnoise was demarcated by a rampart or *vallum*.[7] Further midland expansion, as well as increasing secularisation, is evidenced by the pitched battles fought by Clonmacnoise against Birr in 760 and against Durrow in 764, a clash in which 200 people are said to have died.[8]

From around the year 900, however, the evidence of Clonmacnoise's importance increases. In return for conceding burial rights (which were evidently every bit as sought after in the tenth century as they are today) it received major political patronage from the Clann Cholmáin kings of the Southern Uí Néill. In 909 the high-king, Flann Sinna, financed Abbot Colmán mac Ailella's construction of the *daimhliag mór*, the great stone church which still dominates the ecclesiastical remains on the site.[9] The rectangular open space outside the west façade of this church seems to have been laid out at this time also, as a *platea* or open area with the Cross of the Scriptures placed centrally within it. The inscription on this cross records the names of both Colmán and Flann, whom it styles king of Ireland.[10] The kings of Connacht began to play a powerful role in the affairs of the monastery from the middle of the tenth century, a time when Clonmacnoise also seems to have established close ecclesiastical links with Glendalough.[11] During the eleventh and twelfth centuries the monastery was intimately allied with the Ua Conchobair kings of Connacht and, judging from the surviving remains, this was a period of considerable prosperity. During this time its famed scriptorium produced the *Annals of Tigernach*, the *Chronicon Scottorum*, the *Annals of Clonmacnoise, Lebor na hUidre,* and the collection of annals and genealogies known simply by its shelf number as Rawlinson B.502.[12] Although it was not included among the episcopal sees at the Synod of Ráith Bressail, Clonmacnoise was powerful enough to have its exclusion remedied within months, and at the Synod of Uisneach in 1111 it became the cathedral church of Westmeath. With the coming of the Normans, the monastery appears to have been viewed initially as lying outside the territory granted to Hugh de Lacy, but it was raided by him twice, in 1178 and 1179.[13] After the year 1200, however, several Anglo-Norman lords, in particular William de Burgh, were able to exploit divisions in the succession to the kingship of Connacht and make encroachments on the province. In *c.* 1205 de Burgh devastated Clonmacnoise and, with the building of a castle in 1214, it was absorbed into the Anglo-Norman sphere of influence.[14] After 1210 Athlone became the major crossing-point of the Shannon, and Clonmacnoise gradually declined in importance as the settlement focus shifted upriver.

The layout of monastic towns

A basic problem in the examination of monastic town layout is the fundamental one of the absence of excavation. With the exception of Clonmacnoise, archaeological excavations have not been conducted on the large, open-area scale necessary to recover evidence of urban layout and, as a result, very little is known about the physical appearance of monastic towns. Were they haphazardly arranged, as some writers appear to think, or was there an element of planning in their layout? This question can only be answered by archaeological excavation, and at the moment our evidence for the appearance of monastic towns is drawn essentially from two sites: Armagh and Whithorn. From Armagh there is a range of documentary evidence which enables one to formulate a model of the monastery's appearance, while from Whithorn there is the excavated evidence of a street.

At Armagh the earliest church was established at the foot of the hill on the site known as *fertae martyrum* ('the graves of the martyrs'). The churchmen, however, had their eyes set on a richer prize—the hill summit known as *dorsum salicis* ('the willow ridge'), on which there was a pre-existing fort or a pre-existing sacred site, as the excavations would suggest, particularly when interpreted in the light of the recent evidence from Raffin, Co. Meath.[15] In any event, the church gained control of the hill summit and, in the years that followed, the monastery was laid out on and around this hill. The annals make it clear that the summit was an enclosed area. It is always referred to as the *ráth*, from which it can be assumed that it had defensive elements.[16] Within the *ráth* were the principal churches and shrines of Armagh, the most prestigious burial-places (for kings and those of high status, whether religious or lay), the library and the abbot's house. The position of the *ráth* is indicated today on the west, south and east by the curving pattern of Callan Street and Castle Street, while its location on the north-east is reflected in the arc of a property boundary. The area outside this enclosure was divided into three precincts known as trians. The *trian Saxan* ('English precinct') was located to the north and north-east, where English Street still preserves the name to this day. The *trian masain* ('middle precinct') lay on the south-east, and the *trian mór* ('large precinct') on the west. Annalistic references of 1112, 1121 and 1166 indicate that these trians contained streets and houses which were lived in by students, clerics, shrine-keepers and, probably, craftsmen. The trians formed part of a large outer enclosure, three sides of which are still delimited by Abbey Street, Thomas Street and Ogle Street, but its exact western boundary is unclear. It measured approximately 480m by 360m and would have covered an area of roughly 11.5 hectares (29 acres). It is important to recall, however, that all of this area was not built up, and excavations on the east side of Castle Street have shown that parts remained as open ground and were not built over until the end of the Middle Ages.[17] East of the enclosure, the old churchyard of *fertae martyrum* gradually went out of use as a burial-ground. In the ninth century there were workshops here with evidence for metal-, glass- and amber-working, and in the tenth/eleventh centuries the site was used by a craftsman who manufactured lignite bracelets and articles of jet.[18] An annalistic entry of 1090, which mentions the burning of the stone church of *Na Ferta* together with 100 houses around it, makes it clear that this workshop did not exist in isolation.[19]

The topographical impression provided by this examination of Armagh is that of a settlement divided into three parts: firstly, the hill summit with the major religious buildings—cathedral, round tower and other key churches (many of them probably stone-built), all enclosed within a demarcated area known as the *ráth* (zone 1); secondly, downslope, at the foot of the hill, streets lined with houses and workshops of wood, set within an outer enclosure almost certainly having defensive capabilities, as suggested by the week-long siege of 1103[20] (zone 2); and thirdly, outside this perimeter, on the road leading eastwards and having *fertae martyrum* as its focus, a linear sprawl of suburban houses (zone 3). It is tempting to think that these three zones also reflected the relative social status of their inhabitants, with those of very high status occupying zone 1, those of middling status dwelling in zone 2, and those of low status living in zone 3. Examination of the evidence from Kells reveals a similar pattern, except that the suburb was on the south side in the area known as *Siofíoc*,[21] while the plan of Tuam is almost a replica of Armagh, with an eastern suburb located downhill from the monastic enclosure at Templenaskreen.[22]

The second piece of evidence on the appearance of a monastic town is derived from archaeological excavation in the Hiberno-Norse settlement beside St Ninian's Church at Whithorn in Galloway. This area was colonised by Irish and Hiberno-Scandinavians at the beginning of the eleventh century and it came under the jurisdiction of Dublin for a time.[23] It is arguable, indeed, that the area was colonised from Dublin in order to secure the trade route northwards to Scotland and Scandinavia, another aspect of that Dublin imperialism which caused the colonisation of the Isle of Man, Anglesey and parts of mainland Wales. Excavation immediately south of the churchyard at Whithorn has revealed a street flanked with houses of Hiberno-Norse type.[24] A stratified succession of rectangular houses was uncovered, and their alignment remained focused consistently onto the street throughout the eleventh and twelfth centuries. One of these structures has a particular resonance for anyone familiar with the Irish documentary sources. This is house 7, which produced a range of comb-making debris, including tooth-plate blanks, roughly finished side-plates, antler offcuts and trimmings.[25] It immediately recalls the description of the death of the king of Leinster, Cerball mac Muirecháin (d. 909). An eleventh-century source recounts how, as Cerball rode eastwards into Kildare *ar fud sráite in chéime chloici* ('along the street of the stone step'), a comb-maker advanced from his workshop holding aloft a set of deer antlers. The king's horse took fright at the sight and reared up, unseating Cerball, who fell and was impaled on the upright spear of one of his attendants.[26]

Is it possible, with the evidence available at present, to define the monastic town? I have examined this issue elsewhere, in too great a detail to warrant repetition here,[27] and I have proposed the following working definition, which is based on an analysis of the documentary sources and an examination of the major ecclesiastical centres themselves:

> 'The monastic town is an enclosed settlement, typified by having a major group of ecclesiastical buildings (including dwellings, monuments such as crosses, and ceremonial areas) at its core, lived in by a hierarchically organised society, with a dependent population (generally consisting of craftsmen, students, traders and providers), and which functioned as a political capital and as a focus for regional trade.'

If such an entity is to be recognised on the ground, a number of criteria must be fulfilled. Firstly, there must be evidence for settlement complexity. Typically this could consist of a settlement divided into sectors, with a core of major church buildings, and perhaps having outlying or suburban churches. Secondly, there should be evidence for the presence of domestic houses and workshops; thirdly, evidence for streets and rows of buildings; fourthly, evidence for trade, markets or fairs; fifthly, evidence for enclosure and defence; and sixthly, evidence that the settlement was a political centre. These criteria will now be examined in relation to Clonmacnoise.

Settlement complexity

The settlement core of major churches is still self-evident at Clonmacnoise. The *Daimhliag Mór* or cathedral is essentially a structure of 909; *Teampull Ciarán* may well be contemporary; Temple Kelly is probably the church which replaced the *dearthach* or wooden oratory mentioned in 1167; and Temple Doolin incorporates a small pre-Norman (perhaps eleventh-century) oratory.[28] Temple Connor, Temple Melaghlin, Temple Finghin and the round tower are of twelfth-century date, documentary sources mention the existence of Temple Killin (*Teampull Uí Chilléne*) and Temple Gauney (*Teampull na Gamnaige*), while Temple Espic is known only from post-medieval sources.[29] In addition, there is evidence for the presence of Célí Dé monks, who were most probably tied, as at Armagh, to their own church.[30] Both the scriptorium, for which the first evidence is indirect (the death of the scribe Mac Concumba in 730), and the school, best attested in the eleventh century when there are many references to the *fir legind* of Clonmacnoise, were probably located near these churches.[31] The school was evidently well established by the end of the ninth century, when Suibhne mac Máel Umha was famous enough to be noticed by the *Anglo-Saxon Chronicle* as 'the best teacher among the Scots'.[32] At Armagh the *seniores* or elder brethren had a house within the ecclesiastical core, and their Clonmacnoise counterparts may have been similarly located.[33] Apart from this ecclesiastical core, it is evident that Clonmacnoise was also divided into precincts. In 1082 the eastern *trian* of Clonmacnoise was burnt, a reference which would suggest that there were western and southern trians as well.[34] On analogy with Armagh, these trians were probably located outside the central core of churches. The range of domestic structures and workshop evidence recovered in the recent excavations in the New Graveyard are outside this core and almost certainly formed part of the eastern trian. In 942 the *alith níochtarach* ('lower half') of Clonmacnoise was swept away by a great flood, and while this may be nothing more than a topographical description, it is possible that it refers to a defined sector of settlement bordering the River Shannon on the north of the ecclesiastical core.[35] A short distance to the east of the settlement was the Nuns' Church, first referred to in 1026 although the present building dates to 1167.[36] This may have been the focus for a suburban settlement, as is suggested by the reference in 1082 to the destruction of houses at the churchyard of the Nuns.[37] The river was also an important part of the settlement. Archaeological excavations have revealed a boat slip, and the bridge was clearly a major factor which turned Clonmacnoise into an important crossing-point. This bridge is first mentioned in the documentary sources in 1158,[38] but it is evident from dendrochronological samples recently recovered from the site that a bridge, at least 60m long, was already in existence by 804.[39] In summary, then, the evidence suggests that the layout of Clonmacnoise was broadly similar to that of Armagh, with three zones of settlement—an inner ecclesiastical core, an outer residential area, and a suburban development to the east. It differed from Armagh, however, in that it was located beside a major river, where there were docking facilities and, from at least 804, a major bridge.

Houses and workshops

The reference of 1082, relating to the destruction of houses at the churchyard of the Nuns, is the first documentary mention of houses in Clonmacnoise, although archaeological excavations have revealed structures of earlier date.[40] During the late 1170s the invading Anglo-Normans launched punitive raids on Clonmacnoise from their bases in Leinster and Meath, and the references relating to these raids provide interesting information on structures within the settlement. In the raid of 1178 the *baile* of Clonmacnoise was destroyed, with the exception of the churches and houses belonging to the bishop.[41] The implication is that, as at Kells, Co. Meath, there were private properties within the settlement which were viewed as legitimate spoils, while ecclesiastical property was respected. In the raid of 1179, 105 houses were burnt and, even allowing for some exaggeration on the part of the annalist, it is evident that Clonmacnoise was densely built up by this time.[42] In *c.* 1205 the abbot's fort and 47 houses near it were destroyed.[43] The abbot's fort itself was evidently set apart from the rest of the monastery and, as at Armagh, it seems to have been almost a seigneurial residence. Indeed, as Macalister pointed out, it is quite possible that the later Anglo-Norman castle was built upon the site of the abbot's fort, and it is certainly the case that in 1216 the bishop of Clonmacnoise was compensated by the crown for land which was sequestered from him in order to build the castle.[44] The guesthouse is described in a source which appears to be of ninth-century date as *in castello hospitum*, a phrase which would seem to be a translation of *lios oichid*, and it would suggest that, as at Armagh, the guesthouse was placed within its own enclosure.[45] The archaeological excavations have yielded evidence for the existence of a range of craft activities, including bronze-working, iron-working, leather-working and the manufacture of jet ornaments, while corn-drying kilns are attested by both the documentary and archaeological sources.[46] Fine-quality metalwork was also produced, particularly in the twelfth century, when a school of metalworking appears to have been based at Clonmacnoise.[47] In addition, there was a major stone workshop manufacturing graveslabs and high crosses, and Ó Floinn has shown that it was at its most productive during those periods of peace when it enjoyed the patronage of powerful kings.[48]

Streets

There are three references to streets at Clonmacnoise and the word used consistently to describe them, as at Kells, is *clochán*. In 1026 the paved way (*clochán*) from *Garrdha an*

Banabbad (the abbess's enclosure, i.e. the Nuns' Church) to *Ulnaidh na dtrí gCros* (the mound of the three crosses) was constructed.[49] This is evidently the road connecting the monastery with the Nuns' Church, fragmentary portions of which still exist and which has been described by Macalister.[50] In 1070, MáelCiarán son of Conn na mBocht built a *clochán* from the Cross of Bishop Etchen to the sacristy of St Ciarán's Church.[51] Although its exact position is unknown, it was evidently within the main enclosure. In the same year, 1070, another road (*clochán*) is referred to, stretching from the Cross of Comgall to the mound of the three crosses and from there westward to *Bél na Sráide* ('the entrance to the street'), presumably the eastern entrance to Clonmacnoise where the *sráid* led into the interior of the monastery.[52] Roads were also built across the bog to facilitate access to the monastery. The *Registry of Clonmacnoise*, a late medieval source, credits Fergal ua Ruairc, the king of Connacht who died in 966, with the construction of two causeways or toghers, one of which ran to Clonfinlough.[53]

Trade, markets and fairs

The location of Clonmacnoise on a junction of routeways made it a favourable place for trade both by land and water. In the life of Colmán Ela, Clonmacnoise is described as one of the three chief fairs (*oenach*) of Ireland, the others being at Teltown and Lynally, and in a poem on the fairs Clonmacnoise is fêted as the noblest of the three.[54] The commencement date of the fair is unknown, but Doherty has argued convincingly that fairs began to be held at monasteries from *c.* 800.[55] It is clear from the twelfth-century *Aislinge Meic Conglinne* that monasteries were a normal place for buying and selling, and the regularity with which coins have been found at monasteries, including Clonmacnoise, tends to support this view.[56] The presence of coins at Clonmacnoise is particularly interesting in view of the annalistic record that coins were minted there in 1170, but unfortunately no examples survive.[57] The archaeological excavations have yielded a range of evidence for trade. Metals, including gold, silver and bronze, as well as semi-precious stones such as amber and lignite would have to have been obtained from outside the site. Some precious objects are known to have been donated to the monastery but the most likely mechanism for the arrival of raw materials was trade and exchange. Wine was almost certainly imported although Bede tells us that vines grew in Ireland,[58] and the presence of E-ware among the excavated finds, as well as the reference in the Latin life of Ciarán to the presence of *mercatores cum vino Gallorum*, suggests that Clonmacnoise was tied into a regional and inter-regional network of trade.[59] The River Shannon was a major trade route, and the story in the Life of Ciarán of how Senan's robe, the *Cassal Senain*, was miraculously carried by the river from Clonmacnoise to Scattery Island (and back presumably) provides a clear indication that there were connections between the monastery and the river mouth.[60]

Enclosures and defence

Clonmacnoise was an enclosed settlement. Its *vallum* or rampart is first mentioned by Adomnán *c.* 697 and, in origin, it may have been nothing more than a spiritual boundary or an area of sanctuary.[61] The surviving stretch of *vallum*, however, is conspicuously located on the highest point of a ridge to the south of the ecclesiastical complex, where it commands a good view.[62] The reference to the *trian* suggests the presence of an internal division, while both the guesthouse and the abbot's house were placed within their own enclosures.[63]

The political dimension of Clonmacnoise

The political context within which the monastery of Clonmacnoise was founded is difficult to establish. The legend of the meeting in the bulrushes between Ciarán and Diarmait mac

Cerbaill may be dismissed as a literary motif which reflects the political situation of *c.* 900, but unfortunately it tells us nothing about political relationships in the 540s. The major political event in the Irish midlands during the sixth century was the growing apart of the Uí Néill and the Connachta, and it is difficult to think that the foundation of the monastery was entirely unrelated to this development. There are hints that when Clonmacnoise was founded it lay within the kingdom of Maine, which then extended along both sides of the Shannon, but the rise of the Uí Néill in Mide brought the eastern Uí Maine within their ambit and separated them from the western Uí Maine, who gradually fell under the sway of the Connachta.[64] When documentary sources become more plentiful, it is clear that the monastery was situated in the sub-kingdom of Delbna Bethra, which was nominally a *forthuath* subject to the Southern Uí Néill but, as Byrne has pointed out, in practice it must have been an ecclesiastical state ruled by the abbots of Clonmacnoise, who owned much of the best land in an otherwise marshy area.[65] In the course of the seventh century the monastery began to develop as the principal church of Connacht. It has been suggested that this process is evidenced by the memorial slabs which apparently record the names of early Uí Maine and Uí Briúin kings, but this evidence is no longer viewed as reliable.[66] Guaire Aidne, who died in 663, appears to have been the first king of Connacht to be buried there and, associated as it would have been with endowments and patronage, it shows a significant linkage with Connacht interests.[67] Ryan, in his study of the abbots, established that they were drawn from all over Ireland and derived not from the powerful political families but from the *aithech-thuatha*, and he identified them as people of low status who remained true to Ciarán's origins as the son of a carpenter or cartwright.[68] A closer examination of the list of abbots, however, reveals clear political influence. Between 638 and 724, for instance, all of the abbots except two hailed from Connacht, an indication of Connacht's control over the abbatial office.[69] Throughout the seventh century the abbots tended to be drawn from septs like the Uí Maine and Conmaicne Mara, which were tributaries of the kings of Connacht, but in the second half of the eighth century abbots such as Forbassach (d. 771), Murgal (d. 789) and Anaile (d. 799) came from the Uí Briúin and Uí Fiachrach, families which supplied the kings of Connacht. Such connections reflect the increasingly high political profile of the abbots of Clonmacnoise.

There are indications that Clonmacnoise may have helped the Uí Briúin to consolidate their power in Connacht.[70] The closeness of this connection is shown in two ways, firstly by the burial of kings such as Indrechtach mac Muiredaig (king of Connacht 707–23), a key figure in establishing the Uí Briúin as kings of Connacht, who died as a pilgrim at Clonmacnoise, and secondly by the linkage of the dynasty with the Law of Ciarán.[71] The text of the law does not survive, but it is presumed that it was related to the Law of Adomnán, which forbade the killing, injuring or abuse of women, children and clerics. The law was usually proclaimed with some ceremony: the relics of the saint were exposed and venerated, dues were imposed as contributions which recognised the benefits of the law, and fines were stipulated for any infringements. The Law of Ciarán was first imposed on Connacht in 744 by Forggus mac Cellaig.[72] It was proclaimed again in 788 and repeated in 814.[73] The imposition of these laws reflects the increasing secularisation displayed in the battles with Birr and Durrow in 760 and 764, and it has been suggested that the battle between Clonmacnoise and Durrow may have been connected with the burial at Durrow of the first Clann Cholmáin high-king, Domnall Midi mac Murchado, and the consequent loss of revenues which it involved.[74]

After 638 none of the abbots, with the possible exception of Luccreth (d. 753), were drawn from Munster, and when in 827 the vice-abbacy' (*secnapote*) was given to a Munsterman the *Chronicon Scottorum* noted that this was the first time that it had ever occurred. The unfortunate person, Flann mac Flaithbertaig, was drowned in the Shannon ten years later by Cathal mac Ailella, king of Uí Maine, in what was probably a dispute over succession to the abbacy.[75] In recompense the king gave seven churches to Clonmacnoise, but he was successful in keeping Munstermen out of the abbacy. This dispute happened against the background of a resurgent Munster under the leadership of a puritanical prince-bishop, Feidlimid mac Crimthainn (king of Munster 820–47). Feidlimid took advantage of a weakened Connacht to raid Clonmacnoise and Uí Maine on several occasions, most notably in 832 (when he raided Delbna Bethra three times), in 833, when he killed many of the monastic community and burned the termonn 'to the church door', and again in 846, two years after it had been sacked by Vikings.[76] Feidlimid was deeply influenced by the Célí Dé movement and his raids may have been motivated in part by a fundamentalist zeal directed against the worldly ecclesiastics of Clonmacnoise, but there can be little doubt that there were also political motivations behind his attacks and that to assault the monastery was viewed as synonymous with attacking Connacht.[77]

The influence of Connacht began to wane in the second half of the ninth century, and after the death of Feidlimid mac Crimthainn in 847 Clonmacnoise succeeded in gaining the patronage of the new midland power, the Clann Cholmáin (or Uí Máelsechlainn) kings of Mide. Máel Sechnaill mac Máele Ruanaid, high-king of Ireland from 846 until 862, was a benefactor of Clonmacnoise, Durrow and Kinnity, but his burial at Clonmacnoise indicates that by 862 the Clann Cholmáin viewed the monastery as at least *primus inter pares*.[78] Máel Sechnaill's son, Flann Sinna, may have continued the practice of diversifying patronage or even withholding it from Clonmacnoise because the story is told of how, towards the end of the ninth century, the bishop of Clonmacnoise, Cairpre Cromm (d. 904), had a vision in which the spirits of Máel Sechnaill and his *anmchara* (spiritual confessor) beseeched his prayers to escape the pains of purgatory.[79] Cairpre prayed and fasted on behalf of Máel Sechnaill while twelve priests of Clonmacnoise took up the cause of the *anmchara*. After having interceded for a year, Máel Sechnaill was spared the torments and released from purgatory a day before his *anmchara*, owing, it was said, to the excellence of Cairpre's prayers and the superiority of his intercession above that of the twelve priests! Whether Flann Sinna believed any of this or not is unclear, but it was evidently in his interests, both in this life and the next, to have the support of Clonmacnoise. In 900 he secured the allegiance of the new king of Connacht, Cathal mac Conchobair, to his dynasty, and this left him with just one major rival in Ireland, Cormac mac Cuilennáin, the king of Munster, who celebrated the success of his campaign against the midlands and Connacht by spending Christmas of 907 at Clonmacnoise.[80] In the following year, however, Cormac was defeated and killed at the battle of Belach Mughna by Flann Sinna. Flann's success made him the most powerful ruler in Ireland, and he chose to celebrate it in 909 by financing a reorganisation of Clonmacnoise. This resulted in the construction of the *daimhliag mór* and the Cross of the Scriptures, with its inscription commemorating the names of both Abbot Colmán mac Ailella and Flann, 'king of Ireland'.[81] This was a defining moment in the history of the monastery. Three hundred and sixty years after its foundation there was a major reorganisation of the fabric presided over by Ireland's most powerful political leader and by one of Clonmacnoise's most successful abbots, for Colmán was abbot not only of Clonmacnoise but also of Clonard. He was the first to combine these two abbacies, which would have made him the single most powerful ecclesiastical figure in the midlands, and it is doubtful whether he could have combined the two abbacies without the support of King Flann.[82] This combination of church and crown in 909 provides clear evidence that Clonmacnoise saw itself as having a national role to play, rivalling, or indeed surpassing, that of Armagh, Kells and Kildare. The price of political support, however, was land with immunities, and it has been suggested that it was too high a price to pay because it eventually caused the collapse of the Clann Cholmáin.[83]

During the eleventh and twelfth centuries the monastery was intimately linked again with the kings of Connacht. By this time the association of the two was so close that when Ua Ruairc attacked Connacht in 1065 he began by raiding Clonmacnoise.[84] Similarly in 1115, when Toirrdelbach Ua Conchobair wished to impose a punitive peace agreement on Domnall Ua Máel Sechlainn, king of Mide, the summit was held at Clonmacnoise.[85] This political connection between the monastery and the Ua Conchobair lasted until the end of the twelfth century, and both Toirrdelbach Ua Conchobair (d. 1156) and Ruaidrí Ua Conchobair (d. 1198) were buried at Clonmacnoise.[86] The omission from the sees approved by the Synod of Ráith Bressail may indicate that the star of Clonmacnoise was beginning to wane early in the twelfth century, but it is more likely that it was simply a calculated move against his Ua Conchobair rivals by the patron of the synod, Muircheartach Ua Briain, who had in fact raided Clonmacnoise during that year.[87] The omission was quickly rectified, and at the Synod of Kells in 1152 the political identification of Clonmacnoise with Connacht was recognised by assigning the diocese to the province of Tuam.[88]

From this brief review it is clear that Clonmacnoise played a key role in the politics of the midlands from the seventh to the twelfth century. Physically this is expressed by the Cross of the Scriptures, which is not just a work of piety, nor only a reflection of royal patronage, but also a political statement, a physical proclamation of the importance of Clonmacnoise to the exercise of kingship.

Conclusion

It is evident that Clonmacnoise fulfils the criteria identified above as typifying a monastic town. It had settlement complexity, houses, workshops and streets, as well as evidence for trade, enclosure and political importance. The topography itself bore a striking resemblance to that of Armagh. It had an ecclesiastical core, a series of precincts or *trians* within an enclosure, and an external suburb to the east around the Nuns' Church. The layout of Kells and Tuam was broadly similar, and since it is too much of a coincidence to find that monastic towns in quite disparate parts of Ireland had much the same plan, it suggests that the concept of an ideal monastic town plan existed in the minds of the authorities responsible for its layout. Whether this concept also found expression at the level of streets and houses is something which only excavation will resolve. It is worth recalling, however, that the concept of ideal monastic size is found in the ninth-century *Bethu Pátraic*, where St Patrick is said to have laid out his ecclesiastical settlements on a uniform scale, allowing a diameter of 140 feet for the *lis* (enclosure), 27 feet for the *tig mór* (great house or *magna domus*), seventeen feet for the *cúili* (kitchen or backhouse) and seven feet for the oratory (*aregal*).[89] These dimensions are clearly analogous with those listed for domestic houses in the seventh-century *Crith Gabhlach* and which Lynn has shown are reflected in the excavated evidence.[90]

It is striking that so much of the documentary evidence for the existence of a monastic town at Clonmacnoise is concentrated in the eleventh and twelfth centuries, and it is tempting to suggest that this may have been the result of influence from the Scandinavian port towns established in the tenth century. The recent excavations suggest, however, that this date must be stretched backwards in time, perhaps by several centuries, and this constitutes one of the most significant contributions made by archaeological research to the study of town life in Ireland.

Notes
Abbreviations
A. Clon. = D. Murphy (ed.), *The Annals of Clonmacnoise* (Dublin, 1898).
AFM = J. O'Donovan (ed.), *The Annals of the Four Masters* (Dublin, 1851).

AI = S. MacAirt (ed.), *The Annals of Inisfallen* (Dublin, 1951).

ALC = W.M. Hennessy (ed.), *The Annals of Loch Cé* (London, 1871).

A. Tig. = W. Stokes (ed.), *The Annals of Tigernach* (Felinfach, Lampeter, 1993).

AU = S. MacAirt and G. MacNiocaill (eds), *The Annals of Ulster* (Dublin, 1983).

Chron. Scot. = W.M. Hennessy (ed.), *Chronicon Scottorum* (London, 1866).

MIA = S. Ó hInnse (ed.), *Miscellaneous Irish Annals A.D. 1114–1437* (Dublin, 1947).

NHI = F.J. Byrne, A. Cosgrove, J.R. Hill, F.X. Martin, T.W. Moody, D. Ó Cróinín and W. E. Vaughan (eds), *A new history of Ireland* (Dublin, 1976–).

1. C. Doherty, 'The monastic town in early medieval Ireland', in H.B. Clarke and A. Simms (eds), *The comparative history of urban origins in non-Roman Europe* (Oxford, 1985), pp 45–75.

2. *AU*, 548; *AFM*, 548; *Chron. Scot.*, 544; *AI*, 548; an argument for a date of death in 545 is given by John Ryan, 'The abbatial succession at Clonmacnoise', in *idem* (ed.), *Féil-sgríbhinn Eoin Mhic Néill* (Dublin, 1940), pp 492–3, and repeated in his *Clonmacnois: a historical summary* (Dublin, 1973), pp 27–8. A suggested death date of 556 is similarly shaky; see R.A.S. Macalister, *The Latin and Irish lives of Ciarán* (London, 1921), p. 159.

3. K. Hughes, 'The distribution of Irish scriptoria and centres of learning from 730 to 1111', in N.K. Chadwick (ed.), *Studies in the early British church* (Cambridge, 1958), p. 253.

4. '*Festinate ad alia loca pacifica et meas reliquias relinquite quasi ossa arida cerui in monte*', in C. Plummer (ed.), *Vitae sanctorum Hiberniae* (Oxford, 1910), p. 215, cap. xxxii; the Irish life has a variant, 'go and leave my relics as the bones of a deer are left in the sun because it is better for you to dwell with me in heaven than to remain here by my relics': W. Stokes (ed.), *Lives of saints from the Book of Lismore* (Oxford, 1890), pp 132 and 278.

5. D. Ó Cróinín and M. Walsh (eds), *Cummian's letter de controversia paschali* (Toronto, 1988), p. 90, l. 261.

6. L. Bieler (ed.), *The Patrician texts in the Book of Armagh* (Dublin, 1979), p. 142, no. 25, and p. 160, no. 4; Doherty, 'Monastic town', p. 64; D. Ó Cróinín, *Early medieval Ireland 400–1200* (London, 1995), p. 159.

7. A.O. Anderson and M.O. Anderson (eds), *Adomnán's Life of Columba* (London and Edinburgh, 1961), pp 214–15; R. Sharpe (trans.), *Adomnán of Iona: Life of St Columba* (London, 1995), p. 115.

8. K. Hughes, *The church in early Irish society* (Cambridge, 1966), pp 169–70.

9. *AFM*, 904; *Chron. Scot.*, 908; *A. Clon.*, 901; C. Manning, 'Clonmacnoise Cathedral—the oldest church in Ireland', *Archaeology Ireland* **9**, no. 4 (Winter 1995), pp 30–3; see also Manning, this volume.

10. M. Herity, 'The layout of Irish Early Christian monasteries', in P. Ní Chatháin and M. Richter (eds), *Ireland and Europe: the early church* (Stuttgart, 1984), pp 108–9; D. Ó Murchadha, 'Rubbings taken of the inscriptions on the Cross of the Scriptures, Clonmacnois', *Journal of the Royal Society of Antiquaries of Ireland* **110** (1980), pp 47–51.

11. A. S. MacShamhain, 'The "unity" of Coemgen and Ciarán: a covenant between Glendalough and Clonmacnois in the tenth to eleventh centuries', in K. Hannigan and W. Nolan (eds), *Wicklow history and society: interdisciplinary essays on the history of an Irish county* (Dublin, 1994), pp 139–49; *idem, Church and polity in pre-Norman Ireland: the case of Glendalough* (Maynooth, 1996), pp 140–3. There are indications of the existence of a similar arrangement with Inis Cathaigh (Scattery Island): see Plummer, *Vitae sanctorum Hiberniae*, i, pp 208–9, cap. xxii.

12. Doherty, 'Monastic town', p. 65; J.F. Kenney, *Sources for the early history of Ireland: an introduction and guide*, vol. 1: Ecclesiastical (New York, 1929), p. 377; K. Grabovski and D.

Dumville, *Chronicles and annals of medieval Ireland and Wales: the Clonmacnoise group texts* (Woodbridge, 1984); J.V. Kelleher, 'The Táin and the annals', *ériu* **22** (1971), pp 125–7. It has been suggested, however, that Rawlinson B.502 may have been produced at Kildare: see A.P. Smyth, *Celtic Leinster* (Blackrock, 1982), pp 103–4.

13. *AFM*, 1178, 1179.

14. *A.Clon.*, 1205, 1213; *ALC*, 1214.

15. C. Gaskell-Brown and A.E.T. Harper, 'Excavations on Cathedral Hill, Armagh, 1968', *Ulster Journal of Archaeology* **47** (1984), pp 109–60; C. Newman, '"Sleeping in Elysium"', *Archaeology Ireland* **7**, no. 3 (Autumn 1993), pp 20–3.

16. For this and the summary account of Armagh that follows see J. Bradley, 'The role of town plan analysis in the study of the medieval Irish town', in T. R. Slater (ed.), *The built form of western cities* (Leicester, 1990), pp 39–59.

17. C. Lynn, 'Recent archaeological excavations in Armagh city: an interim summary', *Seanchas Ard Macha* **8**, no. 2 (1977), p. 278.

18. C. Lynn, 'Excavations at 46–48 Scotch Street, Armagh, 1979–80', *Ulster Journal of Archaeology* **51** (1988), pp 69–84.

19. *AU,* 1090.

20. *AFM*, 1103; *AU*, 1103; *ALC*, 1103.

21. A. Simms, 'Früformen der mittelalterlichen Stadt in Irland', in W. Pinkwart (ed.), *Genetische Ansatze der Kulturlandschaftsforschung: Festschrift für Helmut Jäger* (Wurzburg, 1983), pp 27–39; A. Simms and K. Simms, *Kells* (Irish Historic Towns Atlas 4; Dublin, 1990); A. Simms, 'Kells', in J.H. Andrews and A. Simms (eds), *Irish country towns* (Cork, 1994), pp 21–33.

22. P. Gosling, 'Tuam', in J.H. Andrews and A. Simms (eds), *More Irish country towns* (Cork, 1995), pp 119–31.

23. B.E. Crawford, *Scandinavian Scotland* (Leicester, 1987), p. 100; F.J. Byrne, 'Onomastica 2: Na Renna', *Peritia* **1** (1982), p. 267; cf. T.W. Moody, F.X. Martin and F.J. Byrne (eds), *A new history of Ireland*, vol. ix, p. 466 and n. 2.

24. P. Hill, *Whithorn 2: excavations 1984–1987, interim report* (Whithorn, 1988), pp 13–21.

25. *Ibid.*, p. 19; *idem, Whithorn 3: excavations 1988–1990* (Whithorn, 1990), p. 23.

26. J.N. Radner (ed.), *Fragmentary Annals of Ireland* (Dublin, 1978), pp 166–7, and see the comments of Doherty, 'Monastic town', p. 67.

27. J. Bradley, *The medieval Irish town* (forthcoming).

28. Manning, 'Clonmacnoise Cathedral'; R. Berger, 'Radiocarbon dating of early medieval Irish monuments', *Proceedings of the Royal Irish Academy* **95C** (1995), pp 169–70; *AFM*, 1167. Accounts of the monuments are provided by T.J. Westropp, 'A description of the ancient buildings and crosses at Clonmacnois, King's County', *Journal of the Royal Society of Antiquaries of Ireland* **37** (1907), pp 277–306; C. Manning, *Clonmacnoise* (Dublin, 1994); C. O'Brien and P.D. Sweetman, *Archaeological Inventory of County Offaly* (Dublin, 1997), pp 89–95.

29. O'Brien and Sweetman, *Inventory of County Offaly*, pp 89–93; C. Manning, 'The date of the round tower at Clonmacnoise', *Archaeology Ireland* **11**, no. 2 (Summer 1997), pp 12–13; J. O'Donovan, 'The registry of Clonmacnoise with notes and introductory remarks', *Journal of the Royal Society of Antiquaries of Ireland* **4** (1856–7), pp 458–9.

30. P. O'Dwyer, *Céli Dé: spiritual reform in Ireland 750–900* (Dublin, 1981), pp 25–7.

31. *AFM*, 724; *AU*, 730; *A.Clon.*, 727; *scribae*, however, usually translated as scribe, may simply mean scholar. Máeloena mac Olbrann, *fear leighinn* of Clonmacnoise, who died in 857 (*AFM*, 855), is the first of many to be mentioned. See the attempt at a prosopography of Clonmacnoise made by R.A.S. Macalister, *The memorial slabs of Clonmacnois, King's County: with an appendix on the materials for a history of the monastery*

(Dublin, 1909), pp 128–40; Ryan, *Clonmacnois*, p. 17; K. Hughes, 'The distribution of Irish scriptoria and centres of learning from 730 to 1111', pp 243–69.

32. M.J. Swanton (ed.), *The Anglo-Saxon Chronicle* (London, 1996), p. 82; Dorothy Whitelock, however, gave the translation as 'best scholar among the Irish', *English Historical Documents c. 500–1042* (London, 1955), p. 184. The Old English word used to describe Suibne is *lareow*, which is normally translated as teacher, master or preacher. In the Irish sources Suibhne is described as scribe and anchorite: *AFM*, 887; *AU*, 890; cf. Macalister, *Memorial slabs of Clonmacnois*, p. 45, no. 237, and pp 97–8.

33. Stokes, *Book of Lismore*, p. 131; Plummer, *Vitae sanctorum Hiberniae*, p. 214.

34. *AFM*, 1082.

35. *AFM*, 940.

36. *AFM*, 1026; *Chron. Scot.*, 1024; *A.Clon.*, 1026; *AFM*, 1167.

37. *AFM*, 1082; *A.Clon.*, 1080.

38. *A.Clon.*, 1158.

39. D. Boland, C. Breen, A. O'Sullivan, G. Woods, F. Moore and D. O'Hara, 'Clonmacnoise Bridge Project: report of pre-disturbance survey', unpublished report by Irish Underwater Archaeological Research Team prepared for National Monuments Service, Dublin, 1995; D. Boland, A. O'Sullivan and C. Breen, 'An Early Christian wooden bridge on the River Shannon at Clonmacnoise, Co. Offaly', *Newswarp: the newsletter of the Wetland Archaeology Research Project* **20** (November 1996), pp 23–5; O'Brien and Sweetman, *Inventory of County Offaly*, pp 124–5.

40. *A.Clon.*, 1080.

41. *AFM*, 1178.

42. *AFM*, 1179.

43. *A.Clon.*, 1205; cf. *AU*, 823, 1116; A. MacDonald, 'Notes on monastic archaeology and the Annals of Ulster', in D. Ó Corráin (ed.), *Irish antiquity: essays and studies presented to Professor M. J. O'Kelly* (Cork, 1981), p. 310.

44. Macalister, *Memorial slabs of Clonmacnois*, p. 152; H.S. Sweetman (ed.), *Calendar of documents relating to Ireland 1171–1251* (London, 1875), no. 694; cf. F. Henry, *Irish art in the Romanesque period 1020–1170 AD* (London, 1970), pp 36–8; O'Brien and Sweetman, *Inventory of County Offaly*, pp 136–7.

45. W.W. Heist (ed.), *Vitae sanctorum Hiberniae* (Brussels, 1965), p. 232, cap. 29; for the date see R. Sharpe, *Medieval Irish saints' lives: an introduction to Vitae Sanctorum Hiberniae* (Oxford, 1991), p. 392; cf. MacDonald, 'Notes on monastic archaeology', p. 311.

46. H.A. King, 'Excavations at Clonmacnoise', *Archaeology Ireland* **6**, no. 3 (1992), pp 12–14; Plummer, *Vitae sanctorum Hiberniae*, p. 204, cap. xii.

47. Henry, *Irish art in the Romanesque period*, pp 39, 49–50, 100–1; P. Harbison, 'A lost crucifixion plaque of Clonmacnoise type found in County Mayo', in H. Murtagh (ed.), *Irish midland studies in commemoration of N. W. English* (Athlone, 1980), pp 24–38; R. Ó Floinn, 'Schools of metalworking in eleventh- and twelfth-century Ireland', in M. Ryan (ed.), *Ireland and Insular art A.D. 500–1200* (Dublin, 1987), pp 179–87.

48. R. Ó Floinn, 'Clonmacnoise: art and patronage in the early medieval period', in C. Bourke (ed.), *From the Isles of the North: early medieval art in Ireland and Britain* (Belfast, 1995), pp 251–60. (Reprinted in this vol., Chapter 8.)

49. *AFM*, 1026; *Chron. Scot.*, 1024; *A.Clon.*, 1026.

50. Macalister, *Memorial slabs of Clonmacnois*, p. 152; see also P. Harbison, *Pilgrimage in Ireland: the monuments and the people* (London, 1991), p. 144, and O'Brien and Sweetman, *Inventory of County Offaly*, p. 94.

51. *AFM*, 1070.

52. *Ibid.*

53. O'Donovan, 'Registry of Clonmacnoise', p. 452.

54. C. Plummer (ed.), *Bethada Náem nérenn* (Oxford, 1922), i, p. 178; ii, pp 171–2.

55. C. Doherty, 'Exchange and trade in medieval Ireland', *Journal of the Royal Society of Antiquaries of Ireland* **110** (1980), pp 81–4.

56. K. Meyer (ed.), *The vision of Mac Conglinne* (London, 1894), pp 8–9; R. Hall, 'A check list of Viking-age coin finds from Ireland', *Ulster Journal of Archaeology* **36–7** (1973–4), pp 71–86.

57. *A. Clon.*, 1170. The bracteates identified by R.H.M. Dolley, *Sylloge of Hiberno-Norse coins in the British Museum* (London, 1966), pp 142–5, as possible Clonmacnoise issues were subsequently attributed by him to a mint at Waterford: 'The identity of the second (?) Hiberno-Norse mint in Ireland', *Irish Numismatics* **16** (1983), pp 121–4.

58. Bede, *Historia ecclesiastica gentis Anglorum*, cap. i.

59. Plummer, *Vitae sanctorum Hiberniae*, i, p. 214, cap. xxxi. The incident is described somewhat differently in the Irish life—*tucad telcoma lan d'fin othra tire Franc* ('a cask full of wine was brought from the lands of the Franks')—and it adds that a fragment of the cask was kept at Clonmacnoise until recent times; see Stokes, *Book of Lismore*, pp 131 and 276. Wine served from the *Fraochán Ciaráin* (presumably a ministerial chalice) is specifically mentioned in 1118: see *MIA*, *sub anno*; cf. C. Thomas, '"Gallici nautae de Galliarum provinciis"—a sixth/seventh century trade with Gaul, reconsidered', *Medieval Archaeology* **34** (1990), pp 1–26, esp. pp 4 and 21; Ó Corráin, *Ireland before the Normans*, pp 68 and 71–2.

60. Stokes, *Book of Lismore*, pp 128 and 273–4.

61. Anderson, *Columba*, pp 214–15; Sharpe, *Columba*, p. 115.

62. Contrary to the statement by Sharpe, *Columba*, p. 261, n. 62, a substantial stretch of the southern *vallum* survives. Its position is shown by C. Thomas, *The Early Christian archaeology of North Britain* (Oxford, 1971), p. 29. The eastern stretch of *vallum*, however, which Thomas shows taking a right-angle turn before linking up with the eastern boundary of the New Graveyard, does not exist. Manning has recently expressed doubts about the date of the surviving stretch of *vallum*; see O'Brien and Sweetman, *Inventory of County Offaly*, p. 95.

63. *AFM*, 1082; *A. Clon.*, 1205; Ryan, *Clonmacnois*, p. 11; see above, note 38.

64. Byrne, *Irish kings and high-kings*, p. 92.

65. *Ibid.*, p. 221.

66. *Ibid.*, p. 92; Hughes, 'Distribution of Irish scriptoria', p. 253; see C. Swift, 'Dating Irish grave slabs: the evidence of the annals', in C. Bourke (ed.), *From the Isles of the North: early medieval art in Ireland and Britain* (Belfast, 1995), pp 245–9.

67. R.I. Best, 'The graves of the kings at Clonmacnois', *ériu* **2** (1905), pp 164–5; G. Petrie and M. Stokes, *Christian inscriptions in the Irish language,* 2 vols (Dublin, 1872), i, pp 76, 80; but see the comments of Kenny, *Sources*, p. 383, and of Ó Floinn, 'Clonmacnoise: art and patronage', p. 251, on these comparatively late sources; cf. Byrne, *Irish kings and high-kings*, p. 241. The story of Ciarán's birth in Connacht, which has all the appearance of a literary device, probably dates from this time.

68. Ryan, 'Abbatial succession', p. 507; *idem, Clonmacnois*, pp 57–8; cf. Byrne, *Irish kings and high-kings*, p. 171.

69. The exceptions were Crónán Becc (abbot 686–94) and Osséne Frémaine mac Galluist (abbot 694–7); see *NHI* ix, p. 247.

70. Byrne, *Irish kings and high-kings*, p. 248.

71. *Ibid.*

72. *AU*, 744; *A. Tig.* [= *AU*, 743]; hagiographically the *rapprochement* between Clonmacnoise and the Uí Briúin is reflected in the literary device used to bring about Ciarán's birth at

Magh Aí, the centre of Uí Briúin power in Connacht; see Plummer, *Vitae sanctorum Hiberniae*, i, p. 200, and Stokes, *Book of Lismore*, pp 120 and 265.

73. *AU*, 788, 814; *AFM*, 783; *A.Clon.*, 785; *Chron. Scot.*, 814; Byrne states that the law was also proclaimed in 775 after the Uí Briúin defeated the Uí Maine (*Irish kings and high-kings*, p. 252).

74. Ryan, *Clonmacnois*, p. 39; Smyth, *Celtic Leinster*, p. 89.

75. *AFM*, 834; Byrne, *Irish kings and high-kings*, p. 222; the story of how Ciarán was rescued from slavery by a member of the Déisi would seem to indicate the existence of some sort of friendly relations between Clonmacnoise and Munster: see Plummer, *Vitae sanctorum Hiberniae*, i, p. 203, cap. xi, and Stokes, *Book of Lismore*, pp 122 and 267.

76. *AU*, 833; *AFM*, 831, 832, 844; *A.Clon.*, 830, 843; *Chron. Scot.*, 832, 833, 846.

77. Byrne, *Irish kings and high-kings*, pp 228–9.

78. D. Ó Murchadha and G. Ó Murchú, 'Fragmentary inscriptions from the West Cross at Durrow, the South Cross at Clonmacnoise and the cross of Kinnitty', *Journal of the Royal Society of Antiquaries of Ireland* **118** (1988), pp 53–66; cf. L. de Paor, 'The high crosses of Tech Theille (Tihilly), Kinnitty, and related sculpture', in E. Rynne (ed.), *Figures from the past: studies on figurative art in Christian Ireland in honour of Helen M. Roe* (Dun Laoghaire, 1987), pp 153–5; P. Harbison, 'The extent of royal patronage on Irish high crosses', *Studia Celtica Japonica* **6** (1994), pp 77–105; K. Meyer (ed.), 'Das ende von Baile in Scail', *Zeitschrift für Celtische Philologie* **12** (1918), p. 235.

79. J. O'Donovan, J.H. Todd and W. Reeves (eds), *The Martyrology of Donegal: a calendar of the saints of Ireland* (Dublin, 1864), pp 66–7.

80. *AFM*, 895; *AI*, 907; the summit took place at Athlone, not Clonmacnoise as stated by Byrne, *Irish kings and high-kings*, p. 266.

81. See above, notes 9 and 10.

82. Hughes, *Church in early Irish society*, p. 219; L.M. Bitel, *Isle of the saints: monastic settlement and Christian community in early Ireland* (Ithaca, 1990), pp 148–9. In making the link-up with Clonard, Clonmacnoise slipped into a role which had previously been played by Kildare and Armagh; see K. Hughes, 'The cult of Finnian of Clonard from the eighth to the eleventh century', *Irish Historical Studies* **9** (1954–5), pp 18–19.

83. Byrne, *Irish kings and high-kings*, p. 269; for an example of Clann Cholmáin land grants to Clonmacnoise see P. Grosjean, 'Notes d'hagiographie Celtique 17: un miracle posthume de S. Ciarán de Cluáin en faveur du roi Diarmait mac Cerrbeoil', *Analecta Bollandiana* **69** (1951), pp 96–102.

84. *AI*, 1065.

85. *MIA*, 1115.

86. *AFM*, 1156; *A.Tig.*, 1156; *AFM*, 1198. The body of Ruaidrí Ua Conchobair was subsequently placed in a stone shrine: *AFM*, 1207; cf. Best, 'The graves of the kings at Clonmacnois', pp 164–5.

87. *AFM*, 1111.

88. A. Gwynn, *The Irish Church in the eleventh and twelfth centuries* (Dublin, 1992), pp 247–8; cf. *NHI* vol. ix, pp 102 and 277, n. 11.

89. K. Mulchrone (ed.), *Bethu Phátraic* (Dublin, 1939), p. 141; cf. W. Stokes (ed.), *The Tripartite life of St Patrick,* 2 vols (London, 1887), i, pp 236–7.

90. C.J. Lynn, 'Houses in rural Ireland A.D. 500–1000', *Ulster Journal of Archaeology* **57** (1994), pp 81–94.

Clonmacnoise cathedral (photo: Dúchas, the Heritage Service)

7. CLONMACNOISE CATHEDRAL

Conleth Manning

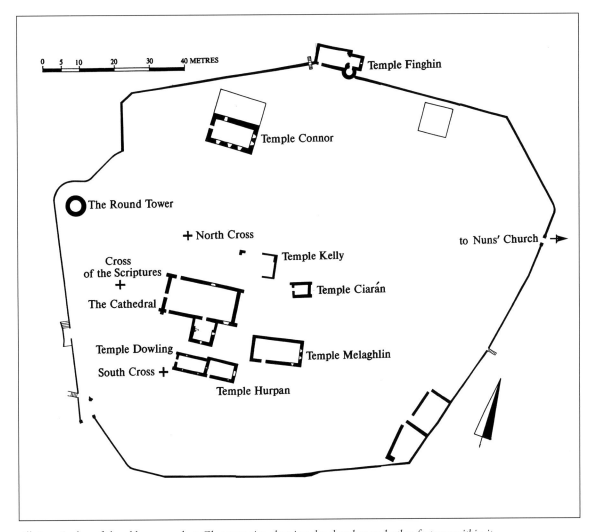

Ill. 1— A plan of the old graveyard at Clonmacnoise, showing the churches and other features within it.

The building known today as the cathedral at Clonmacnoise is the largest of the churches that survive at this important ecclesiastical site (Ill. 1 and frontispiece). It consists of a simple rectangular church measuring 18.8m by 8.7m internally, with antae at all four corners and an attached sacristy with accommodation above on the south side. While the side walls of the building stand mostly to their full height, the east and west walls are badly ruined and survive to only a fraction of their original height. The church was no doubt known by different names at different times. On the earliest maps of the site, dating from the seventeenth and eighteenth centuries, it is called Temple Mac Dermot or Mac Dermot's Church, and it was apparently also known as Mac Coghlan's Church. Its use as a cathedral in the modern sense would probably only have begun in the twelfth century, when Clonmacnoise was made a diocese as part of the reform of the Irish Church. As argued below, it was originally known simply as the *daimliag* or stone church of Clonmacnoise.

The earliest serious commentary on the architecture of the church is that by Petrie,

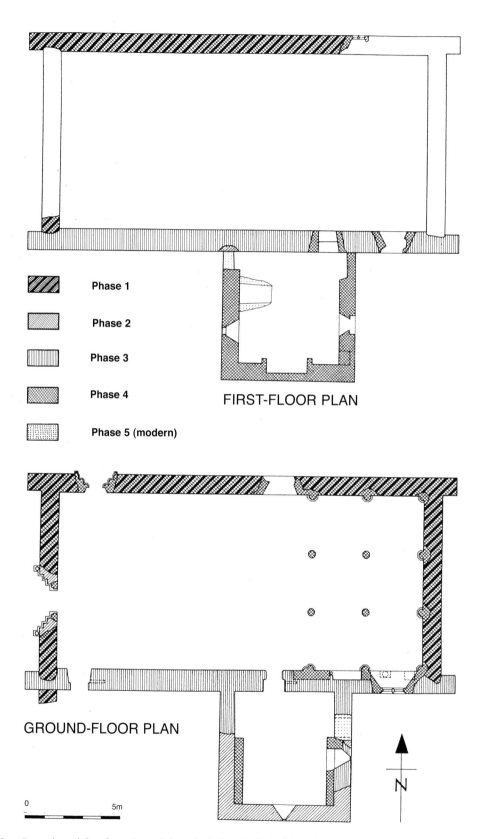

Phase 1

Phase 2

Phase 3

Phase 4

Phase 5 (modern)

FIRST-FLOOR PLAN

GROUND-FLOOR PLAN

0   5m

N

Ill. 2—Ground- and first-floor plans of the cathedral with the building phases indicated.

writing in the middle of the nineteenth century. He accepted the date of AD 909 for the building of the church from the *Chronicum Scotorum* but thought that the west doorway was partly original (Petrie 1845, 271, 275). On the evidence of the *Registry of Clonmacnoise,* he argued that the church was re-edified by Tomultach Mac Dermot, chief of Moylurg, in the early fourteenth century; he saw the pointed arch of the west doorway as being of this date but not the capitals, which he thought were original (*ibid.,* 275). He correctly dated the north doorway to the fifteenth century.

Macalister (1909, 143–4) refers to this church having been originally founded in 904, 'but owing to its many burnings and pillagings it is unlikely that the present structure contains any part of the original building, although it must be noticed that it displays the characteristic antae at all four corners. In any case all the architectural features are insertions, some of them of quite late date.' He described the west doorway as Romanesque and dated the north doorway, with its inscription mentioning Dean Odo, to about 1460, when he assumed the vaulting over the east end of the church was also inserted. Clapham (1952, 17–18) was the only one to publish a detailed plan of the church, in which are shown two major phases of construction: (1) twelfth-century and earlier, and (2) later medieval. In his opinion the presence of antae 'seems to imply that it has preserved its 10th-century plan, though most of the superstructure has been rebuilt'.

Leask was the first to note the unusual proportions of the building, its length–breadth ratio being a little over 2 to 1. As he knew that early Irish churches generally were closer to 1.5 to 1 in length–breadth ratio, this aspect of the Clonmacnoise building puzzled him and he was, as a result, uncertain about its dating (Leask 1955, 72). Henry (1967, 47), in reference to the church built by Flann and Colmán, regarded it as being 'probably on the site of the present cathedral but only its foundations survive below the more recent walls which follow the same plan'. There was also an opinion that the walls might incorporate part of the early tenth-century church but no details were given (de Paor 1960, 33; Killanin *et al.* 1989, 108). Radford (1977, 3) proposed that the present cathedral plan was that of 908. His plan, however, became further removed from reality in that the west doorway was moved to a central position in the west gable. Unfortunately he also used the dimensions of this plan as a basis for his conjectural plan of the wooden church at Kildare as described by Cogitosus in the seventh century (Radford 1977, fig. 1). More recently Hare and Hamlin (1986, 131) thought that most of the fabric, with its roughly coursed rubble masonry and regular system of putlog holes, was of one period but doubted that it was as early as 908. They thought it just as probable that the annalistic references to the completion of roofing of the church around 1100 indicated the date of the earliest phase of the building. Almost all commentators on the building refer to the west doorway as being Romanesque or late Romanesque.

There are two peculiarities of the building on which no one, to date, appears to have commented. These are that the west doorway is off centre (Ill. 4) and that at the south-west corner the remains of a wall can be seen at ground level continuing the line of the west gable southwards (Ill. 5). The only published plans, which are somewhat inaccurate and at a small scale (Anon. 1906–7, 2; Macalister 1909, frontispiece; Clapham 1952, fig. 2), show both features. Clapham's plan is derived from the OPW drawing which Macalister used. Both of these features, along with a change in the masonry of the east and west walls of the sacristy (Ill. 6), indicate that the original south wall of the church was 2m further south than its surviving replacement. This would leave the west doorway central to the original west gable (Ill. 3). We also have a time-frame for the rebuilding of the south wall because it post-dates the original sacristy but pre-dates the inserted vaulting at the east end of the cathedral. The rebuilding and relocation of the south wall is the key to understanding the building and its phases of construction, which are described in sequence below.

Phase 1

This phase is represented by the greater part of the north wall, apart from the top 1.6m and the north doorway and window, as well as the surviving portions of the east and west walls, apart again from later features such as the west doorway (Ill. 7; Ill. 2). The phase 1 masonry is almost exclusively of yellow/brown sandstone, horizontally laid. Many of the stones used are quite small; they vary between 0.15m and 0.7m in length and between 0.1m and 0.3m in height and are undressed, apart from those forming the corners of the north-west and north-east antae. A notable feature of this masonry is a series of regularly spaced putlog holes which fully penetrate the wall (Ills 4 and 7). During construction these would have held horizontal scaffolding timbers projecting a few feet out from the wall face at each side and tied to tall upright timbers. Planks laid on them would have formed working platforms. When the building was completed the timbers were either cut off at the wall face or pulled out, and the consequent hole was roughly blocked with small stones. Once the wall was plastered these features would no longer have been in evidence. It is only when buildings lose their plaster that the putlog holes again become visible.

Where the east and west walls meet the south wall the primary nature of these gable walls is in evidence, and part of the west wall can be seen at ground level on the south side of the south wall (Ill. 5). The antae on the north side of the building are the only surviving features of phase 1. They project 0.75m and average 0.9m in width, which is the same thickness as the walls. It is reasonable to presume that the present west doorway replaced a phase 1 doorway in the same location, but there is no evidence as to what form it took.

A change in masonry in the east and west walls of the sacristy (Ill. 6) indicates that the original or phase 1 south wall of the church was 2m further south than its replacement. National Monuments Service photographs of the excavations at Clonmacnoise in the 1950s show the remains of this wall uncovered in a cutting outside the west wall of the sacristy (Ills 8 and 9). The phase 1 church, therefore, would have measured internally 10.7m north–south and 18.8m east–west. This would leave the present west door position central

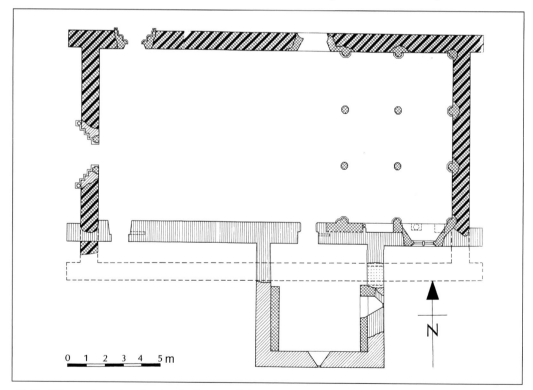

Ill. 3—Ground-floor plan showing the location of the missing original south wall (indicated by dashed line).

Ill. 4—A view of the cathedral from the west, showing the off-centre location of the doorway, the phase 2 upper section of the north anta and the different stonework of the phase 3 south anta.

Ill. 5—The stub of wall running southwards at ground level from the junction of the west and south walls. The west jamb of the south doorway is also visible in this photograph.

Ill. 6—The west wall of the sacristy, showing the modern entrance with gate to the first floor and the blocked-up original entrance in the top left corner. The junction between the phase 2 and phase 3 masonry is arrowed.

Ill. 7—The north wall of the cathedral, showing a regularly spaced series of putlog holes in the phase 1 masonry and the band of phase 2 masonry at the top.

Ill. 8—The original south wall from the west, as uncovered in excavations in the 1950s.

to the west wall of the original phase 1 church (Ill. 3; Manning 1995). The lack of surviving features makes it difficult to date this early phase on architectural grounds, apart from assigning a general pre-Romanesque dating to it.

Phase 2

The surviving fabric indicates that three main features were added to the church in this phase. The present damaged west doorway is a replacement of the original and had a plain pointed arch, as indicated in Blaymires's illustration dating from 1738 (Ill. 10; Ware 1739; Manning 1994b). It is therefore best described as Transitional in style rather than Romanesque. Some of the base and inner jamb stones were replaced in the fifteenth century during phase 4, and the new base stones are carved with foliage ornament of that period (Ill. 11). The doorway has five orders, the outermost of which is a column projecting from the face of the wall. Most of the carved stonework in the doorway is limestone, but the capitals and some of the arch stones are of sandstone. Decoration was confined to the capitals, of which three survive (Ills 12, 13). The innermost one on the north side is a development

Ill. 9—The original south wall from the south, showing external plaster, as uncovered in the 1950s.

Ill. 10—An engraving of the west doorway based on Blaymires's survey of 1738.

Ill. 11—A base on the south side of the west doorway with phase 4 foliate ornament.

Ill. 12—The sandstone capitals on the south side of the west doorway.

Ill. 13—The north side of the west doorway, showing the surviving capital and base of the outer order. The inner capital is modern.

Ill. 14— The south wall of the sacristy, showing traces of the line of the original gable.

Ill. 15—The east end of the south wall, showing the partly blocked sedilia and the truncated piscina and aumbry, all of phase 3, and the window and the remains of the vaulting from phase 4.

Ill. 16— The west wall of Kilmacduagh cathedral, showing the original steeply pitched gable rising in this case from corbels and the later heightening of the side walls, resulting in a lower roof pitch.

of the scalloped form, and the adjacent one has broad, upward-pointing leaves. Both are reminiscent of capitals dating from the later twelfth century at Boyle Abbey, Co. Roscommon (Stalley 1987, 183). The capital of the outer, projecting order on the north side is of the more normal scalloped variety (Ill. 13). The original base of this order also survives and is bulbous, with a leaf or petal device connecting it with each projecting corner of the underlying square plinth (Ill. 13). Parallels for this type of base can be seen in the Romanesque doorway at Killeshin and at the Cistercian abbey of Baltinglass (Stalley 1987, 180). Part of an octagonal column which sits on this base appears to be a later addition. The abacus above the capitals can be seen in Blaymires's and Petrie's illustrations (Ill. 10; Petrie 1845, 275; see also Harbison, this volume) but has not survived.

The original sacristy which belongs to this phase was added to the south side of the early church. It was a single-storey building with its roof ridge running north/south. The line of the gable can still be traced in its present south wall (Ill. 14). The masonry is almost exclusively of roughly shaped limestone blocks and it has two original plain, narrow lancet windows, one in the south wall and one in the east. The latter was moved slightly northwards in phase 3. The northern 2m of the ground-floor section of the east and west walls belong to phase 3, but the doorway (Ill. 15) in the rebuilt south wall of the church is of Transitional style and was part of the phase 2 structure. It is a plain limestone doorway with a pointed arch and a hollow-moulded abacus. The original internal dimensions of the sacristy were 5.3m x 3.75m, which is in the proportion of one to the square root of two.

The third surviving element of this phase is the upper 1.6m of the north wall (Ill. 7). This is limestone masonry similar to that of the original sacristy. This heightening of the original side walls is probably connected with lowering the pitch of the roof in phase 2. Pre-Romanesque churches tend to have steeply pitched roofs (often around 60 degrees). Later building sometimes involved raising the side walls to facilitate the lowering of the roof pitch, as can be seen at the west end of Kilmacduagh cathedral (Ill. 16). Based on parallels, especially for the capitals of the west doorway, this phase could date from the end of the twelfth or early in the thirteenth century.

Phase 3

In this phase a new south wall was built 2m north of the original line, and the sacristy was extended northwards to connect with the new wall (Ills 2 and 3). The stone used in phase 3 is a mixture of sandstone and limestone and is likely to be largely the stone from the original south wall, which would have consisted mostly of sandstone with a band of limestone masonry added at the top in phase 2. Antae were added at the south-west and south-east corners to match the two surviving from phase 1 but the stone used is different from the earlier antae. There are putlog holes also in this wall but, unlike the phase 1 examples, they do not go right through it. There is a doorway at the west end of the wall with a plain segmental arched head, and further east the original doorway to the sacristy was reused in the new wall to give access to the now-extended sacristy. Immediately east of this doorway is the sedilia in the form of two alcoves with pointed arches (Ill.15). East of this again are the aumbry and piscina with a high-level window above, of which only part of the rear arch remains. This was later replaced by the larger phase 4 window which truncated the tops of the aumbry and piscina.

Ill. 17—The fine perpendicular-style north doorway.

One of the main effects of this phase of work was to leave any pre-existing features in the east or west walls off centre. This eccentricity is still a noticeable feature of the west doorway. There is virtually no decorative detail in the work of this phase by which it can be dated. The arches and jambs of the sedilia have a plain chamfer, but the dressing of the stones is reminiscent of work of the later thirteenth or early fourteenth century.

Phase 4

Considerable alterations were made to the building during this phase but its basic plan was not altered (Ill. 2). A very elaborate north doorway in the perpendicular Gothic style (Ill. 17) was added and, as already noted, the west doorway was repaired (Ill. 11). The east end of the church was provided with an elaborate groin-vaulted canopy, three bays wide and two deep, supported by four free-standing columns and eight pilasters (Ill. 18). Decoration was confined to the springing of the vaults, where a sheep's head is carved in one case (Manning 1994a, 15), and the roof bosses, one of which, with a circular panel of foliate ornament, was still on site up to the late 1980s (Ill. 19). A room was

Ill. 18—The east end of the cathedral, showing the remains of the vaulting.

Ill. 19— A decorated roof boss from the vaulting at the east end of the cathedral. This was stolen from the cathedral in the late 1980s.

Ill. 20—The remains of a square masonry platform in the angle between the south wall of the cathedral and the west wall of the sacristy. This platform was associated with the now-blocked first-floor doorway which gave access to the chamber above the sacristy (see Ill. 6).

Ill. 21—The fine phase 4 octagonal chimney with its four side vents.

provided at first-floor level above this vaulting, lit by surviving window openings in the north and south walls. The ground floor of the sacristy was vaulted and a second storey was added above. Access to this level was through a high-level doorway (now blocked up) at the north end of the west wall. Prior to the 1950s, remnants of a square masonry platform survived in the angle below this doorway (Ill. 20). This may originally have been as high as the door threshold, with possibly a wooden stair leading up to it from outside the south wall of the church. The chamber above the sacristy was provided with a fireplace in the south gable wall, and while the head of the fireplace is missing, the fine octagonal chimney above with its cap and side vents survives and is an original feature (Ill. 21). Octagonal capped chimneys, often more ornate than this, are known from the thirteenth to the fifteenth century in England (Wood 1965, 283–8). There are windows at this first-floor level in the east and west walls, and a narrow doorway giving access to the chamber above the vaulted east end of the church. Also of this period is the two-light switch-line tracery window at the east end of the south wall (Ill. 15). The tops of the phase 3 aumbry and piscina were cut off to accommodate this window, while the phase 3 sedilia was mostly blocked up to accommodate the columns of the vaulting.

A mid-fifteenth-century date for this phase is indisputable and is backed up by the inscription on the north doorway which mentions Dean Odo, who died in 1461. Furthermore, a similar doorway at Clontuskert Priory, Co. Galway, bears an inscription dating it to 1471 (Fanning 1976, 102).

Ill. 22—A plaque in the north wall recording the restoration of the building by Charles Coghlan in 1647.

Later work

A plaque in the north wall of the church records that Charles Coghlan, the Catholic vicar-general of the diocese, repaired the building in 1647 (Ill. 22). Apart from this plaque and some contemporary internal plaster, nothing appears to survive from this phase of work.

The OPW plan (Anon. 1906–7, 2) shows a doorway in the east wall of the sacristy at ground level. This is a late feature of uncertain date which was subsequently blocked. The present access to the chamber above the sacristy, which is in the middle of the west wall 2.5m above present ground level, is also of relatively recent date. It is very crudely finished, and on the inside the sloping upper surface of the vault acts as a rough stair giving access to the first-floor level.

Discussion

Phase 1

It is the present writer's contention that phase 1 can be dated exactly to the year 909. References to the building of the *daimliag* of Clonmacnoise occur in only three chronicles: *CS*, where the date printed is 908; *AFM*, where 904 is given; and *AClon*, which has 901.

Ill. 23—A view of the Cross of the Scriptures through the west doorway of the cathedral, illustrating that the cathedral and the cross were carefully aligned.

The 901 dating can be dismissed out of hand as the dating in this late set of annals, which exists only in a seventeenth-century English translation, is often unreliable. The dating in *AFM* up to AD 1020 is out in some cases by up to five years (Walsh 1941, 374). An example of such a discrepancy is the date of the battle of Belach Mugna, which has long been established and accepted as occurring in 908, but is given in *AFM sub anno* 903, indicating a five-year discrepancy. In *CS* Belach Mugna is recorded under the year 907 but, in using *CS*, it is essential to read the introduction, and especially page xlvi, where a table of corrections of between one and four years is given for whole spans of dates. For example, for the printed *CS* dates from AD 905 to 968 the chronology is 'one year in arrear'. All of this points to the conclusion that the building of the church occurred in the year after the battle of Belach Mugna, that is in the year 909. *AClon* further confirms this in that the building of the church is recorded in the entry immediately after that recording Belach Mugna. The actual entry in *CS* is as follows:

Damliag Cluana muc Nois do denem la Flann mac Maoileclainn et la Colman Conaillech. ('The stone church of Cluain-muc-Nois was built by Flann, son of Maelechlainn, and Colman Conaillech.')

The importance of this event is emphasised by the fact that it is repeated in the death notice of Colmán in *AFM* and under the year 925 (*recte* 926) in *CS*:

Colman mac Aililla (.i. do Conaillib Muirtemne; is leis do rinedh Daimliag Cluana muc Nois), Princeps Cluana muc Nois et Cluana Iraird, quievit. ('Colman, son of Ailill (i.e. of the Conaille Muirthemne; it was by him the stone church of Cluain-muc-Nois was made), Superior of Cluain-muc-Nois and of Cluain-Iraird, quievit.')

Clearly the building of the *daimliag* of Clonmacnoise was a major event, and in fact marks the culmination of a successful partnership between Clonmacnoise and the Clann Cholmáin dynasty, in whose territory it lay. Máel Sechnaill, who was of the Clann Cholmáin and who was high-king from 846 to 862, succeeded at times in subduing most of Ireland, making the high-kingship almost a reality (Byrne 1973, 264–5). He was buried at Clonmacnoise (Meyer 1918, 235). Clearly his son Flann, who was high-king from 879 to 916, hoped also to make the high-kingship truly a kingship of all Ireland. To this end, in the year 900 he formed an alliance with Cathal mac Conchobair, king of Connacht, at Athlone when 'Cathal came into the house of Flann under the protection of the clergy of Ciaran' (*AFM, s.a.* 895). In 906 Flann with the king of Leinster ravaged Munster from Gabrán to Luimneach (*AU, CS*). Cormac mac Cuilennáin, king/bishop of Cashel since

902, retaliated most effectively in the following year with a hosting to Mag Léna, where he, leading the Munster forces, defeated the army of Flann (*CS, AI, AFM*). In a second hosting in the same year Cormac took the hostages of Connacht and, according to one account (*AI*), spent Christmas at Clonmacnoise. Flann's fortunes must have been at a particularly low ebb after these humiliations, which makes the defeat and death of Cormac at the decisive battle of Belach Mugna in 908 all the more important for Flann, making his claim to the kingship of all Ireland something of a reality for the first time. Munster was not to recover from this disastrous defeat for many years, and the Eoganacht dynasty, to which Cormac belonged, never fully recovered (Byrne 1973, 266).

Flann's involvement in the building of the *daimliag* at Clonmacnoise should probably be seen as an act of thanksgiving to God for the victory at Belach Mugna and to Colmán, his ally, for his support. To get such a mention in the annals the church must have been large by the standards of the time. Phase 1 of the cathedral, being the largest surviving pre-Romanesque church in the country, is surely the *daimliag* of 909. The fact that there is no reused stone in the phase 1 masonry, which is all uniformly of

Ill. 24— The lower east-facing panel of the shaft of the Cross of the Scriptures, which may depict Abbot Colmán and King Flann, and part of the damaged inscription under it.

sandstone, indicates that this was the first stone building on this particular site. Though the recording of events at Clonmacnoise in the annals in the tenth to twelfth centuries is quite detailed, there is no subsequent reference to the building of a church there which might be equated with phase 1 of the cathedral. Also, the reroofing mentioned in 1104 (*AFM*) is the sort of work that would have been required with a building almost 200 years old: 'The shingles of one half the damhliagh of Cluain-mic-Nois were finished by Flaithbheartach Ua Loingsigh, it having been commenced by Cormac Mac Cuinn-na-mBocht'. Cormac had died the previous year. The 'Eneclar' of the great altar of Clonmacnoise was purchased by Máelsechlainn, son of Domhnall, and a hide was given from each fort in Midhe on account thereof in 1007 (*CS, s.a.* 1005). This has all the appearance of a valuable donation to a pre-existing church, made further understandable by the fact that Flann was Máelsechlainn's great-grandfather. It was probably the venerable-sounding 'altar of Ciaran' beside which Toirdelbach Ua Conchobair was buried in 1156 (*AFM*) and to the north of which his son Ruaidhrí, the last high-king of Ireland, was buried in 1198 (*AFM*) (*ro hadhnaiceadh don taobh tuaidh daltoir theampaill móir Cluana mic Nóis*—'interred at the north side of the altar of the great church of Clonmacnoise').

Another matter relevant to the building of the *daimliag* at Clonmacnoise is the inscription on the Cross of the Scriptures (Ill. 23). While it is badly damaged and only a few letters can be clearly seen, the inscription has been convincingly reconstructed to read as follows (Ó Murchadha 1980; de Paor 1987, 152–3):

OR DO RIG FLAIND MA...MAELSECHNAILL OROIT DO RIG HERENN

73

OR DO COLMAN DORRO..IN CROSSA AR..RIG FLAIND
('A prayer for King Flann, son of Máelsechnaill, a prayer for the king of Ireland, for Colmán, who made this cross for King Flann')

The Flann and Colmán of this inscription are most likely the same two who, according to the annals, built the *daimliag* at Clonmacnoise. While others have made alternative suggestions (de Paor 1987, 154) or have cast doubt on the reading given above (Harbison 1979; 1992a), it is still the simplest and most obvious conclusion. The use of the title RIG HERENN ('king of Ireland') to describe Flann could most appropriately be used after the battle of Belach Mugna and raises the question of whether both the cross and the church were erected at the same time in 909. The position of the cross, directly west of the west door of the cathedral, suggests an association between the two monuments (Ill. 23). Furthermore, the lowest figured panel on the east face of the shaft shows an ecclesiastic and a layman together holding an upright staff, the bottom of which either rests on or is being pushed into the ground (Ill. 24). While scriptural interpretations have been suggested (Stalley 1990, 156–7; Harbison 1992a, 49) they are unlikely, being neither as obvious nor as well known as would be expected on such a prominently placed panel. Also the respective interpretations (Moses and Aaron, and Joseph interpreting the dream of Pharaoh's butler) have no convincing parallels in Ireland. The most common interpretation in the past was that it represented either St Ciarán and Diarmait mac Cerbaill or King Flann and Abbot Colmán. The discovery of a possible though later parallel for this scene on a metal cross from Essen has reopened the discussion and would lend support to the theory that it is Flann and Colmán who are here depicted. This shows Abbess Matilda and Otto, duke of Bavaria and Swabia, reaffirming the faith of the imperial house by together clasping a processional-type cross in a pose similar to that in the scene at Clonmacnoise (Fitzpatrick 1993, 17–18). The story of St Ciarán and Diarmait may also be reflected in this scene. According to the story, the outlawed Diarmait helped Ciarán to erect his wooden church at Clonmacnoise, and Ciarán foretold that Diarmait would be high-king by the following evening. The reigning high-king was killed the next day and Diarmait was proclaimed king in his place (*AClon*, 547). Byrne (1973, 91) has pointed out that this is a late invention by writers at Clonmacnoise. It could very well date from the time of Máelsechnaill or Flann, and it is worth noting that Diarmait was their direct ancestor. A serious problem with the story is a chronological disparity between the accession of Diarmait in 544 (*AU*) and the foundation of Clonmacnoise given under the year 548 in the usually reliable *Annals of Ulster*. Late attempts to reconcile these dates may be responsible for the conflicting dates found in different chronicles for the foundation of Clonmacnoise and Ciarán's death, the latter probably correctly given as 549 in *AU*.

De Paor (1987, 154) has argued that the Colmán mentioned on the Cross of the Scriptures was the artificer who made the cross, and the wording of the inscription certainly supports this interpretation. He further argued that the Colmán mentioned in the inscription on the Kinnitty cross along with Flann's father, Máelsechnaill, high-king from 846 to 862, was probably the same artificer. This theory would support a date not too long after 879 for the Cross of the Scriptures and makes the previously accepted date in the early tenth century highly unlikely. There is, however, one consequence of this theory that is difficult to accept, and that is that Colmán and Flann would have built a major church at Clonmacnoise in 909 while a magnificent cross already stood in front of it with a prominent inscription mentioning Flann and some other obscure Colmán, who carved it.

Some research has recently been published on the legal status of the *saer* or wright in the Early Historic period in Ireland (MacLean 1995). In the oldest legal texts the *saer* is represented as working only in wood, and the different types of wrights are described as those who built wooden churches, millwrights, builders of ships and boats, and those who could make utensils out of yew. Any one of these had the status of a minor noble, but if he mastered three or four of these crafts his status could increase accordingly, and such a 'chief master wright' could have the status of a 'high lord'. Originally other craftsmen, such as metalworkers and even jurists, could not attain this high status. Over the centuries during which these texts were revised the wrights began to work in stone as well as timber and, among other things, the texts mention the erection of stone churches, causeways and crosses as part of the work of the wright. The master wright would not do the actual work but would have the expert knowledge of how to perform the task and would be involved in designing and supervising the work. Of relevance to the making of the high cross is the fact that the relief-carver, who would have done the stone-carving under the direction of the wright, was of considerably lower status, being the equivalent of a strong farmer.

Could it be that Abbot Colmán was also a chief master wright? This would better explain his part in the building of the stone church and why, in his death notice, it is stated so specifically that it was he who had built the church. It is then easier to accept that it is the same Colmán who is mentioned in the inscription on the Cross of the Scriptures as he would truly have made the cross in the sense of having designed it and of having supervised the work. The Colmán mentioned on the Kinnitty cross with Máelsechnaill (high-king from 846 to 862) was probably another wright. Though chronologically unlikely, there is a slight possibility that he may have been the abbot of Kinnitty of that name who was killed at the battle of Belach Mugna in 908 (*AU*). The suggestion that Abbot Colmán of Clonmacnoise was also a craftsman/mason has already been made by Henry (1980, 44–5). She stressed the manual work aspect of Colmán's craftsmanship as in Benedictine practice, rather than the high-status design and supervisory role of a chief master wright which I argue would be more appropriate for this virtual prince of the Church.

The family of Ua Brolcháin produced both prominent ecclesiastics and master wrights in the eleventh and twelfth centuries. One member of the family, Flaithbheartach, was *coarb* of Colm Cille in Derry as well as being a bishop, and he, along with the high-king, Muircertach Ua Lochlainn, built the great stone church of Derry in 1164 (*AU*). It sounds as if he also was a master wright, as was another member of this family, Maol Bhrighde, who died in 1029 (*AU, AFM*). The latter's son, another Maol Bhrighde, died as bishop of Kildare in 1097 (*AU, AFM*). A member of the same family as late as the fifteenth century was involved in building work at Iona, as recorded in an inscription on capitals in the church there (MacLean 1995, 126; Ní Bhrolcháin 1986, 44).

One might also ask whether wrights had more influence at Clonmacnoise than was normally the case in early Irish monasteries. In this regard it is worth remembering that Ciarán's father was a wright and that Ciarán himself, the founder of Clonmacnoise, was often referred to as *mac an tsaoir* ('the son of the wright'). Also, one of the finest of the great collection of cross-slabs from Clonmacnoise is that requesting a prayer for TUATHAL SAER. An unusual feature of the abbatial succession at Clonmacnoise is that it was not dominated by any one family or *tuath* and that many came from the less powerful *tuatha* such as the Conaille Muirthemne, in present-day County Louth, to which Colmán belonged (Ryan 1973, 56–8). Could it be that membership of a profession, such as that of master wright, was more important for advancement at Clonmacnoise in some cases than *tuath* or family affiliations? An abbot called Breasal, who was also of the Conaille Muirthemne, made the paved way (*clochán*) from the garden of the abbess to the Cairn of the Three Crosses in 1026 (*AFM, AClon*). In 1070 (*AFM*) Abbot Maelchiaráin, son of Conn na mBocht, constructed two further paved ways at Clonmacnoise. Were both of these abbots also master wrights?

The dating of pre-Romanesque stone churches in Ireland has been and continues to be problematical largely because these buildings have very few features and little or no decoration. Looking at the annalistic references to stone churches, Peter Harbison (1970, 49) summed up the position well in stating that 'the custom of building churches in stone began to spread in Ireland in the 9th century, became more common during the 10th, and was the standard type by the 11th'. However, it is not possible in our present state of knowledge to distinguish the earlier from the later examples or to establish the relative date of any particular feature. Some of the features which are commonly thought of as being typical of these pre-Romanesque churches are (1) antae (projecting side walls) or corbels at the corners which allowed the roof to be carried over the gables, (2) lintelled doorways centrally placed in the west wall, (3) simple small windows (often round-headed), one in the centre of the east wall and one towards the east end of the south wall, (4) the use of large stones in the masonry, (5) steeply pitched gables, and (6) internal length to breadth ratio of around 1.5 to 1. Most of these are discussed by Leask (1955, 49–60). A feature of many early churches is a projecting plinth at ground level, often protruding only from the exterior face (Manning 1981/2, 208). Another feature of the masonry of some early churches and round towers is the occurrence of putlog holes, noted by Hare and Hamlin (1986, 131, 136–7) at Clonmacnoise cathedral and some round towers such as Roscam, Co. Galway. It could not, of course, be used alone as an indicator of date because it is a feature of more recent buildings, being especially common in thirteenth- and fourteenth-century masonry in Ireland.

A series of radiocarbon dates from the mortar of selected early churches (Berger 1995) has raised some questions about the dating of these churches. However, without a series of dates for each building and details of the exact source of the sample in each case it is difficult to be confident of the results of this work for a particular building. The only church at Clonmacnoise which was dated in this campaign is Temple Ciarán. This is the smallest of the churches at the site and measures only 3.8m by 2.8m internally. Its deep antae and sandstone masonry with putlog holes are very similar to phase 1 of the cathedral and the two buildings would seem to be roughly contemporary. The calibrated date range for it is AD 660–980 (at 95% confidence level) based on a residue of charcoal in the mortar (Berger 1995, 169–70). This would support the dating of phase 1 of the cathedral to 909.

If the 909 date is accepted, what implications has it for the dating of pre-Romanesque churches? Unfortunately no doorway or windows survive from this phase and no indication of the roof pitch. It could be inferred that deep antae are an indicator of early date and that ordinary masonry with putlog holes may be just as early as the so-called Cyclopean masonry which is found in many pre-Romanesque churches. The latter, which usually consists of large thin stones set on edge to form the facing of the walls, is a sophisticated building technique which requires a strong mortared core for stability. It also requires suitable stone, such as the type of limestone found on the Aran Islands. The early portion of Temple Dowling, immediately south of the cathedral at Clonmacnoise, is built mostly of limestone in a version of the Cyclopean style, with relatively large stones set on edge forming the wall facing. The original antae were shallow in comparison with those on the cathedral and Temple Ciarán, which might indicate that it is of later date. The original doorway does not survive at Temple Dowling but at Temple Ciarán the northern half of the doorway appears to be original. It is of dressed sandstone without orders or rebate and the start of a plain semicircular arch can be seen at the top. There is no evidence that this was an insertion or later feature. If the dating argued above is correct, this round-headed doorway may be as early as 900 and is likely to be earlier than most lintelled doorways. A strange feature of it was the portion of a cross reused in the lower courses of its jamb (Ill. 25) (removed by the OPW in the 1950s). Again there is no reason to believe that it was not originally there as it certainly would have been very difficult to insert it subsequently. This is referred to as the upper part of a shaft in Harbison's corpus (1992a, 56, catalogue no. 57), and on one face is a pair of confronted lions with interlocking jaws. There has been some disagreement about the dating of the fragment, with some scholars claiming a date of around 800 on the basis of parallels in the Book of Kells (Hicks 1980, 16) and others suggesting a date in the Romanesque period (Edwards 1984, 59). The context of this stone being built into the original fabric of Temple Ciarán would confirm the earlier dating for this cross fragment.

Putlog holes in Irish pre-Romanesque ecclesiastical buildings were first adverted to specifically by Hare and Hamlin (1986), especially in reference to round towers. The illustration of the south church at Derry, Co. Down, in that article (Hare and Hamlin 1986, fig. 92) clearly shows putlog holes in this small early church with antae. The nave of the cathedral at Glendalough, a large rectangular building with antae, which is almost as large as the phase 1 building at Clonmacnoise, also has putlog holes penetrating the thickness of the walls (Manning 1996). These holes can also be seen high up in the east gable of the nave of St Kevin's Kitchen at Glendalough (Cochrane 1911–12, fig. 26). The early church with antae at Moone, Co. Kildare, has putlog holes in its east gable wall. The churches with antae at Agha, Co. Carlow, and Kilree, Co. Kilkenny, have them in their surviving west gables, and the north church at Monasterboice, though it does not have antae, has putlog holes and is probably basically a pre-Romanesque church, its features being mostly later insertions. It is likely that as people look for these features many more examples in early churches will be discovered. However, it does appear at present that the churches with so-called Cyclopean masonry or versions of it do not have this feature. Putlog holes cannot, of course, be used in themselves as dating evidence, but at least they do not preclude a wall from having an early date.

The internal length to breadth ratio of the phase 1 building is 1 to 1.75 or 4 to 7. This is close enough to be reasonably certain that it is deliberate, and while Leask argued for a ratio of less than 1.5 to 1 for the earliest churches, it is likely that in different cases other ratios of importance would have been used, as in Cistercian abbeys of a later date (Stalley 1987, 75). One to the square root of two (1 to 1.4142) was a common ratio used, but the nave of the cathedral at Glendalough is in the proportion of 1 to 1.62, which is close enough to the golden section (1 to 1.618) (Stalley 1987, 266) to be reasonably certain that this was intentional. It is, probably, best to think of the ratio of Clonmacnoise cathedral as 4 to 7 because both numbers are important in Christian tradition.

Phase 2

This phase is typical of what is known as the transitional School of the West of Ireland, dating from the later years of the twelfth and early years of the thirteenth century. At Clonmacnoise itself Temple Melaghlin and at least the west doorway of Temple Connor are in the same style. The surviving work of this phase in the cathedral is very plain, with only the remaining capitals and one base of the doorway having carved detail (see pp 65, 69). These capitals are variations of the scalloped capital whereby plant forms and foliage have been incorporated, as on capitals in the transept of Boyle Abbey (Stalley 1987, 183). Large elaborate doorways such as that at the cathedral are rare in this style, and the plain orders are probably best paralleled in east-range doorways at abbeys such as Boyle and Ballintober.

In the twelfth century, Clonmacnoise had a close association with the Ua Conchobair kings of Connacht. In 1115 Toirdelbach Ua Conchobair presented three objects to Clonmacnoise: a drinking horn with gold, a silver cup with gold and a paten of copper with gold and silver (*CS*, *s.a.* 1111). Ruaidrí, the father of Toirdelbach, died on pilgrimage at Clonmacnoise in 1118, 26 years after having been blinded and consequently deposed as

Ill. 25—The north jamb of the west doorway of Temple Ciarán from the inside, showing the built-in cross-shaft fragment before its removal in the 1950s.

king of Connacht (*AFM*, etc.). The round tower at Clonmacnoise was completed by Gillachrist Ua Maoileoin and by Toirdelbach Ua Conchobair in 1124 (*CS, s.a.* 1120) (Manning 1997). The objects presented by Toirdelbach Ua Conchobair were among objects stolen from Clonmacnoise in 1129 (*AFM*):

> The altar of the great church [*daimhliag mór*] of Clonmacnoise was robbed, and jewels were carried off from thence, namely, the carracan [model] of Solomon's Temple, which had been presented by Maelseachlainn, son of Domhnall; the Cudin [*Catinum*] of Donnchadh, son of Flann; and the three jewels which Toirdhealbhach Ua Conchobhair had presented, i.e. a silver goblet, a silver cup with a gold cross over it, and a drinking horn with gold; the drinking horn of Ua Riada, king of Aradh; a silver chalice, with a burnishing of gold upon it, with an engraving by the daughter of Ruaidhri Ua Conchobhair; and the silver cup of Ceallach, successor of Patrick.

These objects were recovered in the following year and the thief was hanged. Toirdelbach himself, who at times was the most powerful king in Ireland, was buried beside the Altar of Ciarán at Clonmacnoise in 1156 (*AFM*). Toirdelbach's son, Ruaidrí, the last high-king of Ireland, having abdicated in 1183, died at the monastery of Cong in 1198 and was buried on the north side of the altar of the great church (*teampall mór*) of Clonmacnoise (*AFM*). Some years later, 1207=1208, his remains were disinterred and placed in a stone shrine (*AFM*).

This last reference to the translation of the remains of Ruaidrí Ua Conchobair is found only in the *Annals of the Four Masters* and no further details are given. This, the first step in an attempt to have the last high-kin of Ireland canonised, was no everyday event, but one with considerable political implications. The man who is likely to have been instrumental in this is Ruaidrí's own brother, Cathal Crovderg Ua Conchobair, king of Connacht. He was at the height of his power at this time, his chief rival for the kingship of Connacht, Cathal Carrach Ua Conchobair, having been killed in 1202 'through the miracles of God and St Ciarán' (*AFM*). The latter sentiment is indicative of a common interest between Cathal Crovderg and Clonmacnoise. His other main rival in Connacht, William de Burgo, died in the winter of 1205–6. Cathal Crovderg made an agreement at that same time with King John that he would hold one third of Connacht in fee as a barony and pay tribute for the rest (Otway-Ruthven 1968, 76). The enshrinement of Ruaidrí Ua Conchobair's remains could well have been the context for the phase 2 rebuilding of the cathedral and, if so, Cathal Crovderg is likely to have been the patron. A poem in Irish, written in Cathal Crovderg's time, lists Connacht kings buried at Clonmacnoise (Best 1905). It is likely to have been composed before 1208 and after 1198 because it mentions both Toirdelbach and Ruaidrí lying buried at each side of the altar of the great temple (*tempall mór*). Indeed, it is likely to date to after 1202, when Cathal was unopposed in his kingship. The following verse from this poem indicates how the clergy at Clonmacnoise had fallen on hard times:

'I give thanks to the king of heaven, to God I give thanks, for having come to the king of Tuam, with whom I am, from the paupers of Cluain Ciarán' (Best 1905, 171).

In the later twelfth and very early thirteenth centuries Clonmacnoise had been going through difficult times. After having been one of the wealthiest and most important monasteries in Ireland, it was now becoming one of the poorest and most insignificant diocesan centres (Gwynn and Hadcock 1970, 64–5). According to the *Annals of Clonmacnoise,* Meiler FitzHenry plundered Clonmacnoise in 1200. In 1203 it was again plundered by William Burke (*ALC*), who according to another account plundered it twice within the space of a week (*AClon*). The latter source also records a major fire at 'Liseanabby' at Clonmacnoise, when 47 houses, both great and small, were burnt in the year 1205 (*recte* 1206?). A second garbled sentence refers to the altar presented by Máelseachlainn in the great church apparently being damaged by fire, indicating that the cathedral itself was probably badly damaged. The year 1207 also saw the death of Bishop Cathal Ua Máel Eoin on 6 February (*AClon*), and presumably the succession soon after of Bishop Muiredach Ua Muirecén (Moody *et al.* 1984, 275). This latter bishop is mentioned in a strange document called the *Registry of Clonmacnoise*, which survives only in a seventeenth-century English translation (O'Donovan 1856–7; see also Kehnel, this volume); it lays down the rights of different families to be buried at Clonmacnoise and lists what churches were granted to Clonmacnoise to acquire those rights. There is a lot of contradictory dating evidence in this document, but it could well have been originally drawn up by Bishop Muiredach (his surname is given as O'Muridhe in it) but, if so, certain sections were added at a much later date. According to the *Registry* the following was engraved in Irish on his tombstone: 'Muriertach O Murride Bp of Clone, Head of all Meth. Slanan his foster brother erected this stone monument for him'. This stone was apparently seen by Bishop Dopping in 1684, and he described it as being 'beyond the cathedral at the east end'. Bishop Muiredach may have been attempting to revive the fortunes of Clonmacnoise by having it accepted as the burial-place of prominent Irish families from many parts of Ireland. Having Ruaidrí Ua Conchobair's remains enshrined and the cathedral restored, probably with the help of Cathal Crovderg, could be seen as part of this plan. Bishop Muiredach died in 1214 (*AU, ALC*), and in that same year the castle of Clonmacnoise was built (*ALC*). It is highly unlikely that any of the School of the West work at Clonmacnoise in the cathedral, Temple Melaghlin or Temple Connor would have been done after Norman control was established with the building of the castle in 1214. It is also worth noting that Cathal Crovderg, when he died in 1224, was buried at his own Cistercian foundation of Knockmoy, Co. Galway (*AFM*), presumably because Clonmacnoise was in Norman hands at the time.

Phase 3

The phase 3 work at Clonmacnoise cathedral is difficult to date, but the late thirteenth or early fourteenth century is likely. It was probably necessitated by structural problems, but the solution arrived at—of moving the south wall inwards by 2m—destroyed the symmetry of the building and is unlikely to have been the result of patronage by a chieftain or lord. This is the only phase of work which could possibly have been paid for by Tomaltagh Mac Dermot, lord of Moylurg from 1331 to 1336, who has been associated with work on the cathedral by Petrie (1845, 275) and others (Anon. 1906–7, 5) on the evidence of *The Registry of Clonmacnoise,* which names Tomaltagh Mac Dermot as having 'repayred or built the greate church uppon his owne costs' (O'Donovan 1856–7, 453). There were, however, a number of lords of Moylurg of this name, one dying in 1206 (*AFM*; O'Donovan 1856–7, 452) while another died in 1458. The latter is the more likely person to have given his name to this church by being associated with phase 4 work on the building (see below), though direct evidence is lacking.

Phase 4

A date of about 1460 has been accepted by most commentators for both the north doorway and the vaulting at the east end of the building. The vaulting over and heightening of the sacristy has not, however, been connected with this phase of work, and a date as late as the seventeenth century has even been suggested for it (Harbison 1992b, 277). Functionally the room over the sacristy and that over the vaulting at the east end of the church are closely

Ill. 26—Detail of the figures and inscriptions over the north doorway of the cathedral.

connected. They had a communicating doorway, and probably the only access to the room above the altar was through that over the sacristy.

The inscription on the north doorway (Ill. 26) reads 'DNS ODO DECANUS CLUAN ME FIERI FECIT' ('Lord Odo, dean of Clonmacnoise, had me made'). There can be absolutely no doubt but that this Dean Odo was the 'Dean O'Malone, the most learned man in all Ireland', who 'died at Cluain-muc-Nois-mic-Fidhaigh' in 1461 (*AFM*). Documents at Armagh relating to the year 1460 give his full name and title and show him and the bishop of Clonmacnoise (Seán Ó Dálaigh, OFM) embroiled in a controversy with the abbey of Granard over the rectory of Ballyloughloe (Lynch 1992, 150). Dean Odo, who did not appear when summoned to Drogheda by the archbishop and did not obey other mandates in this matter, was suspended, excommunicated and interdicted while the bishop was only suspended. 'Odo Omolane self-styled dean of Clonmacnoise' was referred to as notoriously contumacious (*ibid.*, 153). The reason they were disobeying the archbishop was that they had already appealed to a higher court, Rome. Early in 1459 Bishop John O Daly, Dean Odo and four canons sent a petition to Pius II, declaring that they had instituted a separate college of four priest-canons, who should be bound to the duty of residence and of singing masses and other divine offices, by day and by night. They had appropriated the rectory of Ballyloughloe in the diocese for the support of the canons because the fruits of the diocesan prebends were not sufficient to maintain the whole body of canons of the chapter. The pope confirmed the institution of the college and the appropriation of the rectory of Ballyloughloe for its support (Gwynn 1946, 150–1).

The first-floor accommodation provided above the sacristy and east end of the cathedral in phase 4 is likely to have been for these four canons living collegiately in part of the building where they were to worship day and night. The north doorway is a masterpiece of late medieval Irish stone carving. The depth and complexity of the mouldings are extraordinary in themselves, while the carving on the outer order of the arch is so intricate as to resemble lace. Biting on the vine-scroll stem in this ornament is an example of a fabulous beast known as an amphisbaena (see Johnson 1987). This two-legged creature has wings and another head at the tip of its tail (Manning 1994a, 24). The three carved figures above the doorway are, from left to right, saints Dominic, Patrick and Francis, each being identified by a separate inscription on the horizontal projecting frame above. St Francis, whose face has long been damaged, and St Patrick are carved in relief on flat plaques, but the stone bearing St Dominic has a raised frame at the sides and base which curves outwards at the top. It looks as if this piece was carved for a specific location elsewhere but not used until this doorway presented an opportunity to employ it. The choice of saints is curious, as is the fact that Ciarán is not represented, but then it must be remembered that Francis and Dominic and the mendicant orders they founded were very popular in medieval Ireland. Also, many of the bishops of this poor diocese of Clonmacnoise had been Franciscans or Dominicans, including Seán Ó Dálaigh, OFM, who was the bishop when the doorway was erected. The central position of St Patrick probably reflected the primacy of Armagh and the fact that Clonmacnoise is in the ecclesiastical province of Armagh.

While Odo himself may have financed the beautiful north doorway, it is likely that a wealthier patron would have been required to finance the rest of the work, especially considering that the diocese was too poor to support a full complement of canons. While any direct evidence is lacking to connect the Tomaltagh Mac Dermot who died in 1458 with this work, he seems a more likely candidate to have given his name to this building than either of his predecessors of the same name. In the first place, he was lord of Moylurg for almost four decades from 1421, at a time when the Mac Dermots were one of the most powerful families in Connacht, easily surpassing the O'Connors, who were much weakened by divisions among themselves (Nicholls 1972, 148). Secondly, the Mac Dermots were a

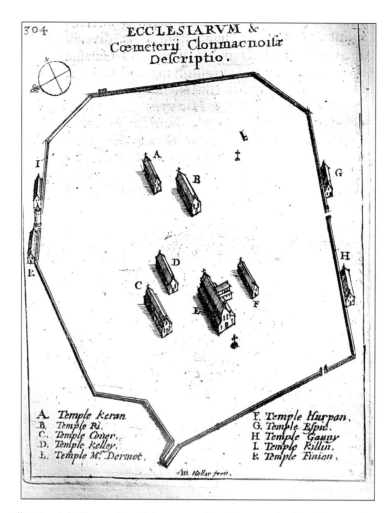

Ill. 27—A bird's-eye view of the graveyard at Clonmacnoise from the second edition of Ware's De Hibernia & antiquitatibus eius disquisitiones *(1658).*

branch of the O'Connors and regarded themselves as equal to them, only ceding their rights to the kingship of Connacht on condition of receiving certain tributes. A bardic poem written in his honour encourages Tomaltagh to revive his rights to the kingship of Connacht as the tributes were not paid by O'Connor, who 'is not thy superior in real power' (McKenna 1939, 123; 1940, 75). Another indication of his importance is that no less than three bardic poems addressed to him survive (McKenna 1939, 123–31; Mac Cionnaith 1938, 415–19). Given this background, Tomaltagh could well have financed most of the phase 4 work at the cathedral in the final years of his life. That this church was the burial-place of some of the most famous kings of Connacht would have been an added bonus. An interest in matters spiritual is indicated by his pilgrimage to Santiago de Compostela in Spain, accompanied by Mairgreag O Carroll, Mageoghegan, O Driscoll, one of the Fitzgeralds, the daughter of O Farrell, and many others, in 1445 (O'Donovan 1846, 211–12). He was not, however, buried at Clonmacnoise but at Boyle Abbey (*AC, AFM*) with his ancestors. A later Mac Dermot, Brian Óg, was buried at Clonmacnoise in 1636, having died of dysentery at Athlone after attending a council there summoned by the earl of Strafford to enquire into landholding in Connacht (*ALC*). This entry claims that twenty lords of his kindred were interred here before him, and O'Donovan (1856–7, 452, n. 7) states that the Mac Dermot chiefs were buried in the cathedral up until the year 1736. However, Boyle Abbey was their burial-place, and there are references to Mac Dermot burials there as late as 1582 and 1589 (*ALC*), long after its dissolution. It was fortified by the English in 1592 (Stalley 1987, 243), which may have left the Mac Dermots without a burial-place and might help to explain the 1636 burial at Clonmacnoise.

Subsequent history

It was recorded in 1547 that 'a great wind arose the night before the festival of St Bridget . . . it threw down churches, monasteries, and castles, and particularly the two western wings [*uilinn*] of the church [*teampall*] of Clonmacnoise' (*AFM*). Maybe these were porch-like structures outside the north and south doors. The same annals record that in 1552 'Clonmacnoise was plundered and devastated by the English of Athlone; and the large bells were taken from the cloigtheach. There was not left, moreover, a bell, small or large, an image, or an altar, or a book, or a gem, or even glass in a window, from the wall of the church out, which was not carried off'. The cathedral was restored for the last time in 1647, during the period of the Confederation of Kilkenny, by the Catholic vicar-general, Charles Coghlan, as recorded on a plaque set into the north wall. However, apart from the plaque itself and some obviously contemporary plaster, no other features survive from this restoration. The building fell into ruin again soon after. Bishop Dopping, writing in 1684, states that 'The structure of this church is very good, and the walls not decayed; it was ruined by the Irish in the late rebellion' (O'Donovan 1856–7, 447). Ware's mid-seventeenth-century plan of the churchyard at Clonmacnoise (Ill. 27), which shows all of the churches roofed (Ware 1658, 304; Manning 1994b), is likely to be based on a sketch-plan with the date October 1621 (British Library Add. MS 4787, 276), which was probably based on an original done for James Ussher, the then newly appointed bishop of Meath (William O'Sullivan, pers. comm.; Manning 1998). By 1689 the vaulting at the east end of the

RUINS OF CLONNACNOIS

Ill. 28—An engraving of Clonmacnoise from the east, from Brewer's Beauties of Ireland *(1826), after an original by Petrie.*

cathedral must already have been broken down because a stone from it is incorporated in the western extension of Temple Dowling built in that year. Blaymires's plan and view of 1738 indicate that the east gable was still standing and had two windows in it somewhat off centre (Ware 1739, opposite p. 165; Manning 1994b). Petrie's views from the 1820s also show the east gable intact (Manning 1994a, 7, 14), while that from the east indicates two openings in this gable. A larger and clearer print of this latter view from Brewer (1826) indicates a centrally placed two-light main east window with simple switch-line tracery like that in the south wall (Ill. 28). It also shows a window at first-floor level in the same wall towards its south side. An attempt to depict both of these windows may explain the two openings in this gable wall shown on Blaymires's plan (Manning 1994b). Petrie (1845, 275) also recorded the damage done to the west door since he first visited the site.

Conclusion

A detailed analysis of this building has revealed four main phases of construction. Historical records clearly indicate a dating and context for two of the phases, 1 and 4. Phase 1, the original stone building, is the largest pre-Romanesque church in Ireland, as well as being the oldest precisely dated church in the country of which a substantial portion survives. It was built by Abbot Colmán and the high-king Flann in 909, the year after Flann's decisive victory over the Munstermen at Belach Mugna. The phase 2 work can be dated, from its transitional School of the West style, to the late twelfth or early thirteenth century. It may be associated with the enshrinement of the bones of the last high-king of Ireland in 1208. Phase 3 involved the rebuilding of the south wall 2m in from its original line in or about the late thirteenth century, probably necessitated by foundation failure or collapse. Phase 4 can be closely dated to the late 1450s and involved major embellishment of the building and the provision of accommodation, over the sacristy and over the east end of the church, probably for a college of four canons established at that time.

Acknowledgements

I would like to thank the following: Gerard Woods for surveying the building and for the finished drawings, and John O'Brien for helping with the survey; John Scarry for the photographs; Heather King, Paul McMahon, David Sweetman and Tadhg O'Keeffe for helpful discussion; Tom Nolan, who was helping me to measure the building when it all began to fall into place; Tom Moore and the guides at Clonmacnoise for their kindness and helpfulness; Liam de Paor for permission to refer to his excavations on the south side of the cathedral in the 1950s; and William O'Sullivan for bringing to my attention the plan dated 1621 in the British Library and for the deduction that it was probably made for Ussher.

References

Abbreviations
AClon = D. Murphy (ed.), *Annals of Clonmacnoise* (Dublin, 1896).
AConn = A. Martin Freeman (ed.), *Annals of Connacht* (Dublin, 1944).
AFM = J. O'Donovan (ed.), *Annals of the kingdom of Ireland by the Four Masters* (7 vols) (Dublin, 1854).
AI = S. Mac Airt (ed.), *Annals of Inisfallen* (Dublin, 1951).
ALC = W. M. Hennessey (ed.), *Annals of Loch Cé* (2 vols) (London, 1871).
AU = S. Mac Airt and G. Mac Niocaill (eds), *Annals of Ulster* (Dublin, 1983).
CS = W.M. Hennessy (ed.), *Chronicum Scotorum* (London, 1866).
JRSAI = *Journal of the Royal Society of Antiquaries of Ireland*.
PRIA = *Proceedings of the Royal Irish Academy.*

Anon. 1906–7 *Clonmacnoise, King's County*. Extract from the 75th Annual Report of the Commissioners of Public Works in Ireland. Dublin.

Berger, R. 1995 Radiocarbon dating of early medieval Irish monuments. *PRIA* **95C**, 159–74.

Best, R.I. 1905 The graves of the kings at Clonmacnoise. *Ériu* **2**, 163–71.

Brewer, J.N. 1826 *The beauties of Ireland*, vol. 2. London.

Byrne, F.J. 1973 *Irish kings and high-kings*. London.

Clapham, A. 1952 Some minor Irish cathedrals. In Memorial volume to Sir Alfred Clapham, being a supplement to *The Archaeological Journal*, vol. 106, for the year 1949, pp 16–39.

Cochrane, R. 1911–12 *Historical and descriptive notes with ground plans, elevations, sections and details of the ecclesiastical remains at Glendalough, Co. Wicklow*. Commissioners of Public Works in Ireland, Dublin.

de Paor, L. 1960 Clonmacnois. In *Programme of the Summer Meeting 1960 at Dublin*, 31–4. Royal Archaeological Institute of Great Britain and Ireland.

de Paor, L. 1987 The high crosses of Tech Theille (Tihilly), Kinnitty, and related sculpture. In E. Rynne (ed.), *Figures from the past: studies on figurative art in Christian Ireland in honour of Helen M. Roe*, 131–58. Dublin.

Edwards, N. 1984 Two sculptural fragments from Clonmacnois. *JRSAI* **114**, 57–62.

Fanning, T. 1976 Excavations at Clontuskert Priory, Co. Galway. *PRIA* **76C**, 97–169.

Fitzpatrick, L. 1993 Raiding and warring in monastic Ireland. *History Ireland* **1** (3), 13–18.

Gwynn, A. 1946 *The medieval province of Armagh 1470–1545*. Dundalk.

Gwynn, A. and Hadcock, R.N. 1970 *Medieval religious houses: Ireland*. London.

Harbison, P. 1970 How old is Gallarus Oratory? A reappraisal of its role in Early Irish architecture. *Medieval Archaeology* **14**, 34–59.

Harbison, P. 1979 The inscription on the Cross of the Scriptures at Clonmacnois, County Offaly. *PRIA* **79C**, 177–88.

Harbison, P. 1992a *The high crosses of Ireland: an iconographical and photographic survey* (3 vols). Bonn.

Harbison, P. 1992b *Guide to the national and historic monuments of Ireland*. Dublin.

Hare, M. and Hamlin, A. 1986 The study of early church architecture in Ireland: an Anglo-Saxon viewpoint. In L.A.S. Butler and R.K. Morris (eds), *The Anglo-Saxon church*, 131–45. Council for British Archaeology, Research Report 60.

Henry, F. 1967 *Irish art during the Viking invasions 800–1020 A.D.* London.

Henry, F. 1980 Around an inscription: the Cross of the Scriptures at Clonmacnois. *JRSAI* **110**, 36–46.

Hicks, C. 1980 A Clonmacnois workshop in stone. *JRSAI* **110**, 5–35.

Johnson, D.N. 1987 An unusual amphisbaena in Galway City. In E. Rynne (ed.), *Figures from the past: studies on figurative art in Christian Ireland in honour of Helen M. Roe*, 233–41. Dublin.

Killanin, Lord, Duignan, M. and Harbison, P. 1989 *The Shell Guide to Ireland*. Dublin.

Leask, H.G. 1955 *Irish churches and monastic buildings 1: The first phases and the Romanesque*. Dundalk.

Lynch, A. 1992 A calendar of the reassembled Register of John Bole, archbishop of Armagh, 1457–71. *Seanchas Ard Macha* **15** (1), 113–79.

Mac Cionnaith, L. 1938 *Dioghluim Dána*. Baile Atha Cliath.

MacLean, D. 1995 The status of the sculptor in Old-Irish law and the evidence of the crosses. *Peritia* **9**, 125–55.

McKenna, L. 1939 *Aithdioghluim Dána*, vol. 1. Irish Texts Society Vol. XXXVII, Dublin.

McKenna, L. 1940 *Aithdioghluim Dána*, vol. 2. Irish Texts Society Vol. XL, Dublin.

Macalister, R.A.S. 1909 *The memorial slabs of Clonmacnoise*. Dublin.

Manning, C. 1981/2 Excavation at Kilteel Church, Co. Kildare. *Journal of the County Kildare Archaeological Society* **16** (3), 173–229.

Manning, C. 1994a *Clonmacnoise*. Office of Public Works, Dublin.

Manning, C. 1994b The earliest plans of Clonmacnoise. *Archaeology Ireland* **8** (1), 18–20.

Manning, C. 1995 Clonmacnoise Cathedral—the oldest church in Ireland? *Archaeology Ireland* **9** (4), 30–3.

Manning, C. 1996 The nave of Glendalough Cathedral. *IAPA newsletter: Bulletin of the Irish Association of Professional Archaeologists* **22**, 6.

Manning, C. 1997 The date of the round tower at Clonmacnoise. *Archaeology Ireland* **11** (2), 12–13.

Manning, C. 1998 The very earliest plan of Clonmacnoise. *Archaeology Ireland* **12** (1), 16–17.

Meyer, K. 1918 Das ende von Baile in Scáil. *Zeitschrift für celtische Philologie* **12**, 232–8.

Moody, T.W., Martin, F.X. and Byrne, F.J. 1984 *A new history of Ireland, vol. IX. Maps, genealogies, lists*. Oxford.

Ní Bhrolcháin, M. 1986 Maol Íosa Ó Brolcháin: an assessment. *Seanchas Ard Mhacha* **12** (1), 43–67.

Nicholls, K. 1972 *Gaelic and Gaelicised Ireland in the Middle Ages*. Dublin.

O'Donovan, J. 1846 The Annals of Ireland, from the year 1443 to 1468, translated from the Irish by Dudley Firbisse, or, as he is more usually called, Duald Mac Firbis, for Sir James Ware, in the year 1666. *The Miscellany of the Irish Archaeological Society*, vol. 1, 198–302. Dublin.

O'Donovan, J. 1856–7 The Registry of Clonmacnoise; with notes and introductory remarks. *JRSAI* **4**, 444–60.

Ó Murchadha, D. 1980 Rubbings taken of the inscriptions on the Cross of the Scriptures, Clonmacnois. *JRSAI* **110**, 47–51.

Otway-Ruthven, A.J. 1968 *A history of medieval Ireland*. London.

Petrie, G. 1845 *The ecclesiastical architecture of Ireland: An essay on the origin and uses of the round towers of Ireland*. Dublin.

Radford, C.A.R. 1977 The earliest Irish churches. *Ulster Journal of Archaeology* **40**, 1–11.

Ryan, J. 1973 *Clonmacnois: a historical summary*. Dublin.

Stalley, R. 1987 *The Cistercian monasteries of Ireland*. London and New Haven.

Stalley, R. 1990 European art and the Irish high crosses. *PRIA* **90C**, 135–58.

Walsh, P. 1941 The dating of the Irish Annals. *Irish Historical Studies* **2** (8), 355–75.

Ware, J. 1658 *De Hibernia & antiquitatibus eius disquisitiones* (2nd edn). London.

Ware, J. 1739 *The whole works of Sir James Ware concerning Ireland, revised and improved* (ed. Walter Harris). Dublin.

Wood, M. 1965 *The English medieval house* (reprinted 1981). London.

8. CLONMACNOISE: ART AND PATRONAGE IN THE EARLY MEDIEVAL PERIOD*

Raghnall Ó Floinn

Introduction

Clonmacnoise, Co. Offaly, belongs to a small group of high-ranking monasteries, such as Armagh and Kells, which developed into centres of ecclesiastical and political power during the early Middle Ages. Its importance derived to a large extent from its position close to the geographical centre of Ireland where the overkingdoms of Connacht, Munster and the Southern Uí Néill met. At a local level it lay on the borders of several minor kingdoms and from them some of its monastic officials were drawn. Its position on the major routeway of the River Shannon ensured its economic prosperity.

The wealth of documentary evidence which survives for Clonmacnoise—no less than three of the series of annals: *Clonmacnoise, Tigernach* and the *Chronicum Scotorum* were actually compiled there—as well as other texts allows us a unique glimpse of the background against which the surviving sculpture, architecture and metalwork associated with the site can be placed.

Artistic activity at a site such as Clonmacnoise, whether it be the carving of a high cross, the building of a new church or the acquisition of new relics or altar plate must have had a historical context involving patron, artist and ecclesiastical official. Recent work on the inscriptions on some of the Irish high crosses by de Paor (1987) and Harbison (1993) have shown the importance of the patronage of the Southern Uí Néill dynasty of Clann Cholmáin kings in the development of the scripture crosses. This paper will attempt to address aspects of art and patronage at Clonmacnoise as revealed by the archaeological and historical sources. Two of these are given particular attention. The first is royal burial and its implications for the dating of the large number of memorial slabs preserved at Clonmacnoise—a body of evidence which, surprisingly, has received little attention from modern scholars. The second is the evidence for the relics of the founding saint and the recorded gifts of altar plate made over the centuries, especially those where the donor's name is known.

A consideration of all the evidence suggests that artistic activity at Clonmacnoise may be divided into three phases.

Phase I: Connacht patronage

The earliest period of the monastery's history is obscure (Ryan 1973, 25–58). The annals and other sources are largely silent and little archaeological evidence earlier than about the mid-eighth century survives—except that being revealed by the ongoing excavations, most recently the discovery of a mutilated ogham stone perhaps pre-dating the monastery's foundation in the sixth century (Manning and Moore 1991). Evidence of fine metalworking in the form of clay moulds, crucibles and bone motif-pieces from levels dating perhaps to the seventh and eighth centuries indicate craft activity at the site from an early date (King 1992a).

It is not clear when royal burial at Clonmacnoise began. The first king recorded in a contemporary annal as being buried there is Guaire Aidne, king of Connacht (*AC 659 recte*

---

*Reprinted from C. Bourke (ed.), *From the Isles of the North: early medieval art in Ireland and Britain* (Belfast, 1995), 251–60.

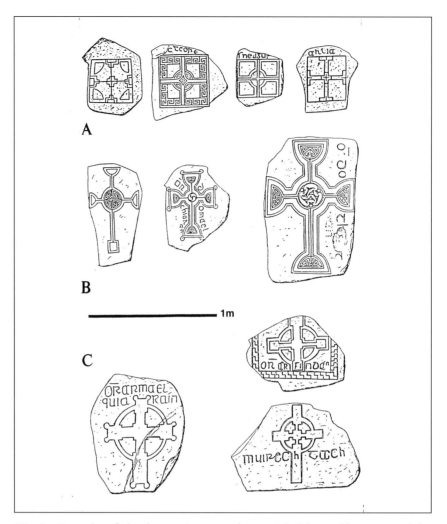

Fig. 1—Examples of the three main types of memorial slabs at Clonmacnoise (after Macalister 1909).

663). At this time Armagh had not yet attained its pre-eminent position in the Irish church and indeed Tírechán, Patrick's biographer, complains of the encroachment by Clonmacnoise on many of Armagh's properties after a recent plague, probably that of 664–8 (Bieler 1979, 42, 142–3). Clonmacnoise was one of a number of Irish monasteries which occupied a position similar to that which the cathedral church of St Denis held in France as the burial place of royalty. This is shown by the existence of several texts on the kings buried at Clonmacnoise. However, their potential for identifying and dating the surviving memorial slabs requires further study (Kenney 1929, 383). Burial of royal persons in a monastery brought with it certain privileges and substantial endowments.

From the early eighth century onwards all the available evidence suggests that the monastery was under the control of successive kings of Connacht. Indrechtach, a king of Connacht of the Uí Briúin Aí, died in 723 at Clonmacnoise and was most likely also buried there (*AU*). That Clonmacnoise appears to have been firmly within the sphere of influence of the kings of Connacht by the mid-eighth century is attested by their proclamation of St Ciarán's *Law* throughout the province in 744, 775, 788 and again in 814. As Hughes noted (1966, 168), such acts normally included a circuit of the saint's relics. In all the cases cited, the kings belonged to the Uí Briúin Aí, the sept who held the kingship of Connacht for most of the eighth and ninth centuries. Their only serious rivals for the kingship came from the Uí Fiachrach, and at least one of the latter who held the kingship, Guaire Aidne (†663), is known to have died and been buried at Clonmacnoise (Byrne 1973, 241). The fortunes of both king and monastery were therefore intertwined—the former gaining spiritual legitimacy for his position, the latter a powerful protector. Any king with ambitions to control the province of Connacht had therefore to earn the favour of and, presumably, to endow Clonmacnoise, the most prestigious church within his sphere of influence (Byrne 1973, 252).

Given the above pattern, it is probable that the earliest datable memorial slab from Clonmacnoise is that of another of the Uí Fiachrach kings of Connacht, Ailill ua Dúnchada, known as Ailill Medraige, whose death is recorded in 764 (Fanning and Ó hÉailidhe 1980, 7, fig. 2.2; Doherty 1991, 63). The language of the inscription (which reads *Ailill aue Dunchatho*) also suggests an early date. Although belonging to the northern Uí Fiachrach, his soubriquet suggests that he was fostered in the territory of the Medraige on the eastern shore of Galway Bay (Byrne 1973, 249). The identification is also strengthened by the fact that this is one of the most elaborate memorial slabs of its type and the only example which includes a patronym.

The slab in question, with several others, was formerly in the graveyard of the Franciscan friary at Athlone, but there are compelling reasons for thinking that it was removed thence from Clonmacnoise. Firstly, there is no historical evidence for an early foundation at Athlone; secondly, all the Athlone slabs are highly decorated. This suggests that they are an antiquarian collection which includes a single example of each of the major Clonmacnoise types as well as part of what is probably the most elaborately decorated memorial slab from early medieval Ireland (Fanning and Ó hÉailidhe 1980, fig. 2.1–4). Thirdly, all except one of the other slabs of the type to which that of Ailill Medraige belongs are provenanced to Clonmacnoise. Finally, there is independent evidence that many slabs were removed from Clonmacnoise to Athlone in the late seventeenth century by Lt Col. Caulfield, governor of Athlone (O'Donovan 1857, 447).

The 'Athlone' slab is therefore of considerable importance as it may be the only independently dated example of a type which is, with the exception of a single example from Gallen, Co. Offaly (Kendrick 1939, fig. 4), exclusive to Clonmacnoise.

The type (hereafter called Type A) typically consists of an equal-armed Greek cross, sometimes ringed, set in a rectangular or square frame, the margins often bearing a meander pattern—otherwise they are undecorated (Fig. 1A; Table 1). The slabs are only roughly dressed and average 50 x 75cm. Of the 272 or so slabs from Clonmacnoise listed by Macalister, 51 are of Type A, representing some 19% of the total (Macalister 1909, nos 34–73, 215–16, 218, 220, 226, 229–30, 232–4, 248). (Although the number of slabs at Clonmacnoise now numbers about 700 (Edwards 1990, 170), Table 1 shows how the proportions of the main classes have remained roughly the same in the fifty years between Petrie's survey (1872) and that of Macalister (1909).) A significant number of Type A slabs lack inscriptions, perhaps as many as one-third (Table 2). Two-thirds certainly bear inscriptions which consist almost universally of a name without qualification, sometimes preceded by a cross. The formula *or(oit) ar/do,* 'pray for', occurs only twice (Macalister 1909, nos 54, 226). The inscription usually occurs outside the frame.

Petrie (1872, 12–14) and Lionard (1961, 157–69 (with a chronological list compiled by Françoise Henry)) dated the slabs at Clonmacnoise by matching the names they bear with those of known abbots. Thus a date range for the production of Type A slabs of *c.* 750 to *c.* 900 can be deduced from their lists. Macalister was more cautious in identifying the names on the slabs with known individuals but pointed out that slabs engraved with a Greek cross in a square frame (equivalent to Type A) *might*, on the basis of the persons named, be assigned to the second half of the eighth century (1909, 103–4). There is, however, no reason to link abbots specifically with these slabs and in any event many of the names which occur are quite common and the use of patronyms is rare. Even unusual spellings of names cannot be used to identify individuals as the name of an individual quite often appears in a variety of spellings in the written texts and, finally, one must also allow for errors in transcription made by the stonemason. Unfortunately, the Petrie/Lionard 'dates' have received widespread acceptance (e.g. Ó hÉailidhe 1967, 121–2; Fanning and Ó hÉailidhe 1980, 17; Mytum 1992, fig. 3:21).

For what it is worth, six of the seven names on Type A slabs which match those of abbots of Clonmacnoise as listed by Lionard fall within the period 751–826 (1961, nos 627–8, 636, 647, 640, 643). But the fact remains that the 'Athlone' slab is the only example that can possibly be dated with any degree of certainty through its inscription, and the type can only be said to be current in the mid-eighth century. The only other dating evidence for Type A slabs is provided by the recent removal of the south cross at Clonmacnoise, underneath which an inscribed slab of this type was discovered (King 1992b, 23). If the south cross does bear the name of King Máelsechnaill mac Máelruanaid (†862) and if it occupied its original position, this would provide a *terminus ante quem* of the mid-ninth century for the slab, and probably much earlier if a memorial slab was being reused as a foundation for the cross. It is also perhaps worth noting that slabs of Type A stand closest to the recumbent grave-markers of Hartlepool and Lindisfarne for which a date from the mid-seventh to mid-eighth centuries is now accepted (Cramp 1984, 98–101, 202–6). Finally, the simple name-only formula and the small size of the slabs might argue for an early date on typological grounds.

It is during the period of currency of slabs of Type A that the earliest carved free-standing crosses appear at Clonmacnoise. This group of crosses comprising the north cross and other fragments from Clonmacnoise as well as outliers in Co. Offaly at Bealin and Banagher, have been dated on a number of grounds to the decades around 800 (Hicks 1980; Edwards 1984). They have their closest parallels with sculpture in Pictland and Dál Riata as does the unusual slab at Gallen, Co. Offaly (Edwards 1990, 164). As the slabs of Type A are also paralleled by some Northumbrian recumbent slabs is it possible that there might be a connection, as yet unclear, between Clonmacnoise and some Columban foundation in the later eighth century which would explain these similarities?

In contrast to dated slabs of the later ninth and tenth centuries, it is significant that Type A slabs are known only from Clonmacnoise and Gallen, the latter probably under the control of Clonmacnoise from at least the early ninth century (Byrne 1973, 221). The cross at Bealin also has an association with Clonmacnoise as the site at Twyford, where the cross formerly stood, has been identified with *Íseal Chiaráin* which is mentioned in the lives of St Ciarán (Cox 1969).

Slab Type	Macalister		Macalister + Petrie	
	No.	% of total	No.	% of total
A	40	19%	51	19%
B	66	32%	80	29%
C	37	18%	46	17%

Table 1—Numbers and percentages of each of the major slab types from Clonmacnoise recorded as extant by Macalister in 1909 (total 207) and the same with the addition of lost slabs recorded by Petrie before 1867 (total 272).

Phase II: Clann Cholmáin patrons

The mid-ninth century would appear to be a watershed in the history of Clonmacnoise. A period of uncertainty is suggested by a dispute among the Connacht kings over the abbatial succession in the early years of the century in which Diarmait Find (†833), king of Connacht, was involved (Ryan 1973, 42–3). The monastery was plundered and burnt on at least nine occasions between 815 and 846 (compared with only three for the previous century). Only two attacks, in 842 and 845, are attributed to the Vikings. The others appear to be by the Irish and in particular by the Munster king, Feidlimid mac Crimthainn, no doubt exploiting the absence of a powerful patron who could protect it. The latter even attempted to impose his own candidate as abbot (Ó Corráin 1972, 98).

The political vacuum created by Feidlimid's death was soon filled by the Clann Cholmáin branch of the Southern Uí Néill, successive kings of which dynasty were, beginning with Máelsechnaill mac Máelruanaid who first comes to prominence in 846, to prove to be the monastery's most enduring patrons and protectors intermittently into the early eleventh century. There is some evidence for Clann Cholmáin interest in Clonmacnoise before Máelsechnaill. In a retrospective annalistic entry under the year 649, but which reflects the polity of the ninth century, it is recorded that Diarmait, son of Áed Sláine, of the Southern Uí Néill, demanded burial at Clonmacnoise in return for a substantial grant of land, which included Lemanaghan (Byrne 1973, 240–1). The battle between the monasteries of Clonmacnoise and Durrow in 764 may well have arisen as a result of a dispute over which of the two was to be the resting place of Domnall, king of Mide (Ryan 1973, 39).

A tenth-century list of the Uí Néill kings, contained in the text *Baile in Scáil*, notes the burial place of fourteen of them over a two hundred-year period from the early eighth to the mid-tenth centuries (Meyer 1901; 1918). Clonmacnoise appears three times: once as the burial place of Áed Allán, a Northern Uí Néill king (†743), and twice as the resting place of the Clann Cholmáin kings Máelsechnaill (†862) and his son Flann Sinna (†916). It was not until Máelsechnaill's death that Clonmacnoise became the burial place of the Clann Cholmáin kings when effective power moved from east to west Mide and both Clonard and Durrow, the burial places of earlier Uí Néill kings, were eclipsed. In addition to Máelsechnaill, his wife Flann, his son Flann Sinna and his daughters Lígach and Muirgal are all recorded as having died or been buried at Clonmacnoise (*AFM* 886, 914, 921, 926). While none of the surviving memorial slabs can be associated with any of the Clann Cholmáin kings, there is now good evidence for ascribing the erection of the south cross and the west cross or Cross of the Scriptures to Máelsechnaill and Flann Sinna respectively (Ó Murchadha 1980; Ó Murchadha and Ó Murchú 1988). Flann Sinna is also credited in the annals jointly with Abbot Colmán with the building of the great stone church at

Slab Type	Inscription formula Name only	Inscription formula *or(oit) at/do*	Frag Inscribed	% Inscribed	Plain	Frag plain
A	26	2	2	67%	7	10[1]
B	1?[2]	46	17	81%	4	12[3]
C	12	26	2	87%	3	3

Table 2—Details of numbers and percentages of inscribed and plain (ie uninscribed) slabs from Clonmacnoise by type, including formula of inscription where known.

91

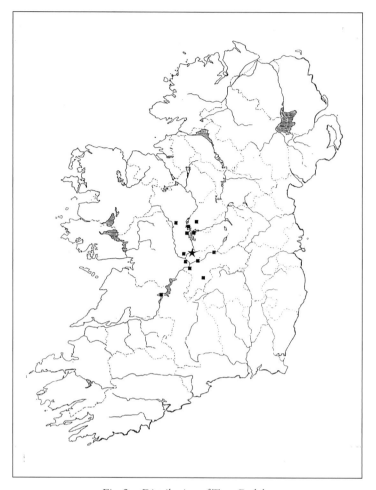

Fig. 2—Distribution of Type B slabs.

Clonmacnoise (*AFM* 904; *AC* 901). The latter work was undertaken immediately after Flann had secured the allegiance of Connacht to his dynasty in the year 900 (Byrne 1973, 266). There is thus a considerable body of evidence for Clann Cholmáin interest in Clonmacnoise.

The second group of datable Clonmacnoise slabs belongs to this period of Clann Cholmáin patronage. This group, here called Type B, consists of slabs bearing Latin (and on occasion Greek) crosses with a central circular expansion and semicircular terminals which are sometimes looped (Fig. 1B; Table 1). They are larger than Type A, measuring on average 1m x 75cm. Macalister lists 80 examples, representing some 29% of the total (1909, nos 126–58, 160–4, 167, 170–5, 177–97, 236–7, 239–41, 243, 251–2, 254, 256, 263–5, 269). Slabs of Type B invariably bear inscriptions, only 4 examples being certainly plain. When inscribed, the *or(oit) ar/do* formula and its variants is almost universal, occurring on some 46 examples (Table 2). There is no instance of an inscription bearing a personal name only— the formula most commonly used on slabs of Type A.

Three Type B slabs can be dated independently on the basis of their inscriptions with some degree of accuracy, two of which are unfortunately lost since Petrie's time. The first is that of Suibne mac Máel Umha, who died in 887 or 892 (Macalister 1909, 97–8). The second is that of Odrán ua Eolais, whose death is recorded in 995 (Macalister 1909, 97). The third can be dated less accurately. This records the name of Dubcenn mac Tadgan, a prince of the neighbouring kingdom of Tethbae and can be dated roughly to the mid-tenth century as his son, Agda, is recorded as dying at Clonmacnoise in 980 (Macalister 1909, 98–9).

Many Type B slabs are decorated with fret and spiral patterns of a type found, for example, on the pinheads and terminals of 'thistle brooches' (Ryan 1983, 150–1) and in manuscripts such as the Book of Mac Durnan (Henry 1967, pls K, L, 43–4) for which a date range of the late ninth to tenth centuries can be proposed. Although variants of this type of slab are known, there is no reason to date any as late as the eleventh or twelfth centuries as proposed by Lionard and others. At present all one can say is that slabs of this type were being made in the period from the later ninth century to the end of the tenth.

Of particular interest is that slabs of Type B, unlike the earlier Type A examples, occur in small numbers within a radius of 25km of Clonmacnoise at sites such as Inisbofin, Iniscleraun, and Rinndown in Lough Ree or more inland as at Gallen and Seir Kieran, Co. Offaly, Fuerty, Co. Roscommon and Ballynakill, Co. Longford (Fig. 2). This may reflect the growing status of Clonmacnoise as a centre of economic activity. Many of these sites can be shown to have been associated with Clonmacnoise and it is reasonable to assume that slabs of Type B were made either at Clonmacnoise or by craftsmen based there. It may even be that the distribution of this type of slab may be used to indicate the extent of Clonmacnoise influence in the midlands during the tenth century.

There are many other forms of memorial slab at Clonmacnoise but these cannot at present be dated with any degree of certainty. The third most common group consists of a ringed Latin cross with rectangular expansions at the centre and at the terminals, here called Type C (Fig. 1C; Table 1). This accounts for some 46 of the 272 slabs recorded by Macalister, representing 17% of the total (1909, 85, 87–9, 91–110, 112, 114–22, 124–5, 210, 212–14, 217, 224, 227, 235, 247). Only 3 are certainly plain. Some 26 use the *or(oit) ar/do* formula, although 12 are inscribed with a single name (Table 2). A few of these are set in frames decorated with a meander pattern and this, combined with the fact that a significant number use the single-name formula, suggests that some may be as early as Type A, although the chronological range of the group cannot be established from the inscriptions. Like the Type B slabs, some occur on sites in the vicinity of Clonmacnoise such as Gallen, Tisaran and Lemanaghan, Co. Offaly, Inisbofin, Co. Westmeath, and Clonfert, Co. Galway. Again, many of these sites are associated with Clonmacnoise.

Contemporary records of the presence of specified relics of St Ciarán at Clonmacnoise do not appear until the end of the ninth century, that is, during the period of Clann Cholmáin patronage. It is, however, likely that many were in existence for a considerable period of time before this.

An unspecified shrine of St Ciarán is recorded as being at Hare Island, Lough Ree, in 894 (*AFM*; *AT*; *CS* 899). This was probably a portable shrine present as a witness to a synod held at the site in that year attended by the bishop of Clonmacnoise. The earliest reference to a specific relic of Ciarán is that known as *Odar Chiaráin*—the hide of St Ciarán's Dun Cow—which is first mentioned under the year 900 when Tadg mac Conchobair, king of Connacht, died after renouncing the world on it (*AI*). Those who died on the hide were believed to have been accorded eternal life. There are other instances of kings dying at Clonmacnoise having been blessed on their deathbeds by relics of the patron saint. For example, Ruaidrí Ua Conchobair, king of Connacht, died in 1118 at Clonmacnoise after receiving communion from the *Fraechan Chiaráin* (*MIA*). This was no doubt a chalice associated with the saint and the record indicates that his relics were part of the burial ritual.

The most important of the bells of the saint, known as *Bearnán Chiaráin*, 'the gapped bell of Ciarán', is first mentioned in 972 (*CS*) and is again mentioned in 1114 (*AT*). It appears that this relic was of sufficient importance to be housed in a church of its own, as the church of the *Bearnán Chiaráin* is said to have escaped burning in 1074 (*AFM*).

Other relics of the saint were kept in a separate structure known as *Erdamh Chiaráin*. The word *erdamh* (*airdam*) has been variously interpreted as a porch, vestibule or sacristy or a small building attached to a larger one (Petrie 1845, 432–8; Macdonald 1981, 308–9; Ó Carragáin 1994, 401, n. 9; O'Keeffe 1995, 267–8). The *erdamh* at Clonmacnoise is first noted in 1070 (*AFM*) and was roofed with slates in 1113 (*CS*). The great gospel book of Colum Cille, it will be remembered, was stolen from the western *erdamh* of the great stone church at Kells in 1007 (*AU*) and it therefore seems reasonable to suggest that the term *erdamh* refers to a small annexe to a larger church building used to keep relics—in effect a treasury.

A crozier of the saint is first mentioned in 930 when it was lost and later recovered from Lough Gara, Co. Sligo (*AFM*; *CS*). The *Annals of the Four Masters* state that it was given the name *Orainech* but this name seems to have been given to another object also associated with St Ciarán (see below).

The donors of the relics of the saint listed above are unknown, but at least two objects which furnished the great altar were given by Clann Cholmáin kings—a cup presented by Donnchad mac Flainn (†944) and an object known as the *Carracán* or 'model' of Solomon's Temple given by Máelshechnaill mac Domnaill (†1022), both of which were stolen in 1129 (*AFM*; *CS* 1125). Donnchad mac Flainn is elsewhere recorded as having enshrined the Book of Armagh (*AFM* 937).

Perhaps the greatest Clonmacnoise treasure was to be found, however, not in the *erdamh* but in the great church itself. In the *Chronicum Scotorum* under the year 1005 (*recte* 1007) reference is made to the purchase of the *eneclair* of the great altar of Clonmacnoise by the last of the Clann Cholmáin kings, Máelsechnaill mac Domnaill (king of Ireland 980–1002, 1014–1022) and 'a hide from every fort in Meath was [given for] it'. The exact meaning of the word *eneclair*, unique to this entry, is unclear. It may be a compound meaning 'front board' or 'face board' [*ainech/enech* + *clár*] (*DIL* 273–4, 119). The only possible explanation of such a word used in the context of an altar (and more particularly a great altar) is that what is meant is an altar-frontal of some kind containing an element of wood. The fact that the object was *purchased* and that a levy was imposed to pay for it is unusual and raises the possibility that it may have been acquired abroad.

Further details on the nature of this altar are to be found in two annalistic accounts of the same event, the capture of Murchad Ua Máelsechnaill, king of Mide, at Clonmacnoise by Tairdelbach Ua Conchobair, king of Connacht, while under the protection of the 'relics and guarantees of Ireland'. These, according to the *Annals of the Four Masters* were:

> *altóir Ciarain co na miondaibh, scrin Ciaráin an óreineach, an Matha mór, an tabb 7 an prióir, 7 dias as gach druing don Eaglaiss. Muiredhach Ua Dubhtaigh an táird epscop, tigherna Connacht, 7 a taoisigh, comharba Phátraicc 7 Bachall Iosa, comharba Feichin 7 clocc Feichin, 7 bóbán Caoimhghin*

> the altar of Ciaran, with its relics; the shrine of Ciaran, called the Oreineach; the Matha-mor [a great gospel of St Matthew kept at Clonmacnoise]; the abbot and the prior, and two out of every order in the Church; Muireadhach Ua Dubhthaigh, the archbishop, the lord of Connaught; the successor of Patrick, and the Staff of Jesus; the successor of Feichin, and the bell of Feichin; and the Boban of Caeimhghin (*AFM* 1143)

In the *Annals of Clonmacnoise* version the same passage reads:

> the alter of St. Querans shrine, Relicks, Norannagh, two prelates of every severall howeses together with Moriegh o'Duffie arch Bishopp of Connaught, primate of Ardmach, the staff of Jesus which St Patrick brought into this kingdom, the coworb of St. ffehin, St. Fehins bell, and the boban of St. Keuin (*AC* 1139).

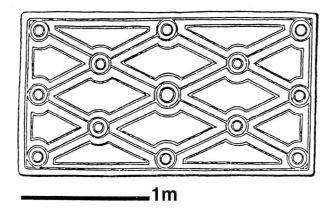

Fig. 3—Stone altar frontal from Glendalough, Co. Wicklow (after Leask, n.d.).

The *Annals of the Four Masters* as translated by O'Donovan imply that the altar contained the relics and that the shrine of St Ciarán was a separate object known as the *Oreineach*. One interpretation was that the altar referred to was a portable altar (Ó Floinn 1997, 265). It is possible, however, that the location of the capture was Clonmacnoise itself, as the Clonmacnoise relics and their keepers—the abbot and prior—are mentioned first. The altar may therefore have been the great altar of Clonmacnoise itself on which the gospel book (*an Matha mór*) was placed and Murchad may have sought sanctuary there. The exact meaning of the two passages is unclear but comparison of the two entries suggests that what was being described was an altar of St Ciarán containing relics (either within it or placed on it) and which was glossed both as the 'shrine of Ciarán' and the *Orainech*. The word *orainech* is a compound meaning either 'face of gold' or 'front of gold' [*ór* + *ainech*/*enech*] (*DIL* 491) and indicates that the object may, in fact, have been a golden altar-frontal or *antependium*. *Orainech* would therefore be a direct translation of the Latin *pallium aureum*—a term used for a golden altar-frontal in the early medieval period, the most important being the *Pala d'Oro* preserved in St Mark's Basilica in Venice.

If the *eneclair* is to be equated with the *Orainech*—both compounds of the same word *ainech*/*enech*—it is almost certain that the great altar at Clonmacnoise was furnished with an *antependium* of wood covered in gold or gilt-copper plates such as that of *c.* 1020 presented by Emperor Henry II to Basel cathedral (Lasko 1972, pl. 130; Caillet 1985, no. 163) or that at Aachen of the same date, given either by Otto II or Henry II (Swarzenski 1967, 44; Lasko 1972, pl. 131). It is significant that the altar was acquired by Máelsechnaill in the year 1007, as this was most probably in response to the donation by his arch-rival Brian Bóruma of twenty ounces of gold on Patrick's altar at Armagh two years previously (*AU* 1005). Was the gold offered by Brian intended perhaps to commission a similar altar-frontal at Armagh? Brian and Máelsechnaill were therefore imitating their continental peers in endowing their favoured foundations with costly altar furnishings, Brian even styling himself *imperator Scotorum* on the occasion of his visit to Armagh (Byrne 1973, 257). Máelsechnaill's interest in promoting Clonmacnoise as an ecclesiastical centre to rival Armagh is further emphasised by the fact that at the time when the altar was acquired, he had installed his brother Flaithbertach as abbot—the only instance of a member of a ruling royal dynasty holding that office.

The destruction at Clonmacnoise in 1205 (*AC*) of a stone altar made by Máelsechnaill mac Domnaill suggests that the altar was still in existence then—perhaps a replacement in

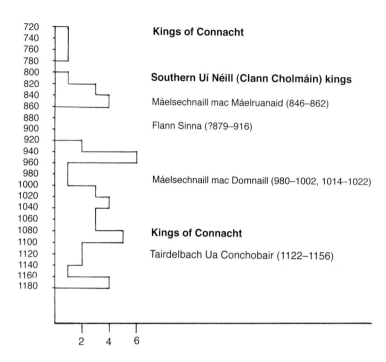

Fig. 4—Number of recorded plunderings/burnings of Clonmacnoise 720–1180 and reigns (as kings of Ireland) of some of its principal patrons.

stone of the earlier wooden altar. Although no trace of the Clonmacnoise altar or its golden frontal survives, possible altar-frontals in stone of eleventh- and twelfth-century date are known from Glendalough, Co. Wicklow (Leask n.d., 44) (Fig. 3) and from Dysert O'Dea (Harbison 1992, 83, figs 262, 264) and Rath, Co. Clare (unpublished). The Glendalough slab is of particular interest as its panelled design of lozenges and bosses is similar to that of the earliest altar-frontals such as the mid-ninth-century *Paliotto* at Milan, that from Aachen of *c.* 1020 (Lasko 1972, pls 48, 131), and some later Danish altar-frontals, in particular that from Lisbjerg of *c.* 1150 (Lasko 1972, pl. 179), and it may well originally have contained painted scenes.

The presence of a golden altar-frontal at Clonmacnoise raises again the question of the function of, and the models used for, the series of bronze Crucifixion plaques, one of which was actually found at or near Clonmacnoise and may well have been made there (Harbison 1980, 26–8, pl. 4; Bourke 1993, figs 21.1a, and 21.2a). A series of square openwork ivory plaques dated to the late tenth century which may have been mounted on an altar-frontal or *antependium* are similar in size to the Irish Crucifixion plaques. These ivories are associated with the endowment of the cathedral of Magdeburg by Emperor Otto I sometime in the 950s or 960s (Brandt and Eggebrecht 1993, 40–8). It is possible that similar ivories, or plaques in other media, adorned the Clonmacnoise altar-frontal and could have provided the inspiration for the series of plaques which Harbison has independently suggested may have been altar decorations (1980, 26). Prominent among the panels of the Aachen altar-frontal of about the same date is a panel of the Crucifixion with attendant angels and soldiers not unlike the Irish Crucifixion plaques (Lasko 1972, pl. 131). A definite Clonmacnoise product of this time is the shrine of the Stowe Missal made by Donnchadh ua Taccáin, a member of the Clonmacnoise community, sometime in the 1020s or 1030s for the monastery of Lorrha, Co. Tipperary (Ó Riain 1991, 295). It bears openwork chequer and cross patterns not unlike the Magdeburg ivories as well as bearing similarities in its figured ornament to the Clonmacnoise Crucifixion plaque (Harbison 1980, 35). The craftsman was in all probability of the same Uí Tadgáin who provided two priests of Clonmacnoise (*AFM* 996, 1168) and perhaps also related to the Uí Tadgáin kings of Tethbae, some of whom were buried at Clonmacnoise (Macalister 1909, 99).

Phase III: renewed Connacht interest

The last group of benefactions to Clonmacnoise are those by several members of the Ua Conchobair family in the early years of the twelfth century. An entry in the *Annals of the Four Masters* under the year 1129 (*CS* 1125) records the theft of a series of precious objects from the altar of the great church at Clonmacnoise and constitutes the fullest pre-Norman inventory of church plate known from Ireland. In most cases the donors of the items are identified. Pride of place is given to the *Carracán* of Solomon's Temple (mentioned above), described as having been presented by Máelsechnaill mac Domnaill (†1022). The next item listed is the *Cudín*—a cup or chalice—of Donnchad mac Flainn, a Clann Cholmáin king who died in 944. At the time of the theft, therefore, this object was nearly 200 years old (hence, perhaps, its relative importance) and had survived the thirty or so plunderings and burnings of the monastery recorded during the intervening period. Next follow three objects presented by Tairdelbach Ua Conchobair, king of Connacht—a silver goblet (*bleidhe*), a silver cup (*copan*) with a gold cross on it (perhaps a ciborium?) and a horn ornamented with gold (*corn go nór*). These three had been presented some years earlier, according to other sources (*CS* 1111; *AFM* 1115). Next is listed the silver chalice and paten presented by the daughter of Ruaidrí Ua Conchobair, king of Connacht (†1118). The chalice was described as *co fforneimh óir fair* (*niam óir fair* in *CS*). This was translated by O'Donovan as 'burnished with gold' but it may be a reference to parcel gilding. There follows another horn which was presented by one of the Uí Riata kings of Arad, a Munster sept located in north Tipperary. The final object, and perhaps the most recent gift, is a silver cup (*copan*) given by Cellach, abbot and archbishop of Armagh (†1129).

The Ua Conchobair donations indicate that by the early twelfth century Clonmacnoise had come under their control. This is confirmed by the fact that all the Ua Conchobair kings of Connacht in the twelfth century were buried at Clonmacnoise. They were also probably responsible for much of the later buildings now visible, including the round tower, completed, according to the annals, by Tairdelbach Ua Conchobair in 1120 (*CS*; *AFM* 1124).

Conclusions

From the evidence of the documentary sources and the surviving sculpture, architecture and artefacts associated with Clonmacnoise it appears that artistic activity was concentrated in a number of short periods when the monastery came under the control of powerful neighbouring overkings. These periods coincide with the burial of the patron and members of his family at the site.

Three principal periods of activity are evident: the later eighth century under the kings of Connacht; the reigns of three Clann Cholmáin kings, Máelsechnaill mac Máelruanaid, Flann Sinna and Máelsechnaill mac Domnaill intermittently from the mid-ninth to the early eleventh centuries; finally, most of the twelfth century under the patronage of successive Ua Conchobair kings of Connacht. Not surprisingly these periods coincide with those of relative peace when few raids were carried out—the monastery being protected by the authority of its patron (Fig. 4). Not a single plundering or burning, for example, is known during the reigns (as kings of Ireland) of Máelsechnaill mac Máelruanaid (*c.* 846–62) and Flann Sinna (*c.* 879–916), only three during the reign of Máelsechnaill II (980–1002, 1014–22; in 985, 1016 and 1020) and three while Tairdelbach Ua Conchobair was 'king with opposition' (1122–56; in 1129, 1135 and 1155).

We must therefore consider that much of the artistic productivity of a large monastery such as Clonmacnoise was probably confined within short periods of perhaps no more than two or three generations at a time—explaining, for example, the significant differences between the two groups of memorial slabs discussed above.

While memorial slabs were probably being produced at Clonmacnoise over the whole period from at least the eighth into the thirteenth centuries, present evidence suggests that the two main types (A and B) may have been made over a shorter period than has been claimed hitherto. What is striking about the slabs is the absence of significant variants within the groups, which would argue in favour of a short period of production for each. There may even have been periods when no slabs were being carved. For example, only five of Macalister's slabs (1909, nos 204–7, 260) have the trapezoidal shape of later grave slabs characteristic of the twelfth and thirteenth centuries.

This localised production over short time spans would account for the fact that slabs may occur in large numbers at some centres but may be absent from neighbouring sites. Further evidence for such localised and periodic carving of memorial slabs comes from sites such as Peakaun (Waddell and Holland 1990) and St Berrihert's Kyle (Ó hÉailidhe 1967), Co. Tipperary, and Inis Cealtra, Co. Clare (Macalister 1916). These have all produced large numbers of slabs, each site having its own distinctive form and design. There is little similarity in slabs between sites (for example, there is only one slab of Clonmacnoise Type B at Inis Cealtra). Those at Peakaun are likely to be early (perhaps seventh or eighth century?), given the absence of the *or(oit) ar/do* formula on inscribed examples and their rough, undressed form, while the majority of those at Inis Cealtra are likely to date from the eleventh century to judge from their expanded inscriptions and elongated, dressed shape.

The evidence from Clonmacnoise and elsewhere cautions against generalising about the effects of, say, the Viking raids on artistic activity at monastic sites. Each must be examined separately to establish the local conditions within its region at a given time.

Notes

1. The majority of these probably were never inscribed.
2. There is some uncertainty as to whether this slab, now lost, did employ the formula *or(oit) ar/do* (Macalister 1909, no. 237).
3. The majority of these fragments are so small that they cannot be said to be from uninscribed slabs.

Acknowledgements

I would like to thank Dr Edel Bhreathnach for much useful discussion and Dr Colmán Etchingham for drawing my attention to the language of the 'Athlone' slab.

References

AC = Murphy, D. (ed.) 1896 *The Annals of Clonmacnoise*. Dublin.

AFM= O'Donovan, J. (ed. & trans.) 1856 *Annala Rioghachta Eireann, Annals of the Kingdom of Ireland by the Four Masters, From the Earliest Period to the year 1616*, 7 vols (2nd edn). Dublin.

AI=Mac Airt, S. (ed. & trans.) 1951 *The Annals of Inisfallen (MS. Rawlinson B. 503)*. Dublin.

AT=Stokes, W. (ed. & trans.) 1993 *The Annals of Tigernach*, 2 vols (repr). Felinfach.

AU=Mac Airt, S. & Mac Niocaill, G. (eds & trans.) 1983 *The Annals of Ulster (to A.D. 1131)*. Dublin.

Bieler, L. (ed. & trans.) 1979 *The Patrician texts in the Book of Armagh (=Scriptores Latini Hiberniae* 10). Dublin.

Bourke, C. 1993 The chronology of Irish Crucifixion plaques. In Spearman, R.M. and Higgit, J. (eds), *The Age of Migrating Ideas, Early Medieval Art in Northern Britain and Ireland,*

175–81. Edinburgh/Stroud.

Brandt, M. and Eggebrecht, A. (eds) 1993 *Bernward von Hildesheim und das Zeitalter der Ottonen, Katalog der Ausstellung*, Bd 2. Mainz am Rhein.

Byrne, F. J. 1973 *Irish Kings and High-Kings*. London.

Caillet, J.-P. 1985 *L'Antiquité Classique, le Haut Moyen Âge et Byzance au Musée de Cluny*. Paris.

Cox, L. 1969 Íseal Chiaráin, the low place of St. Ciarán, where it was situated? *Old Athlone Soc J*, 1, 1 (1969), 6–14.

Cramp, R. 1984 *Corpus of Anglo-Saxon Stone Sculpture*, vol. I, 2 parts, *County Durham and Northumberland*. Oxford.

CS= Hennessy, W. A. (ed. & trans.) 1866 *Chronicum Scotorum*. London.

De Paor, L. 1987 The high crosses of Tech Theille (Tihilly), Kinnitty, and related sculpture. In Rynne, E. (ed.), *Figures from the Past, Studies on Figurative Art in Christian Ireland in Honour of Helen M. Roe*, 131–58. Dún Laoghaire.

DIL= Royal Irish Academy 1983 *Dictionary of the Irish Language* (compact edn). Dublin.

Doherty, C. 1991 The cult of St. Patrick and the politics of Armagh in the seventh century. In Picard, J.-M. (ed.), *Ireland and Northern France AD 600–850*, 53–94. Blackrock.

Edwards, N. 1984 Two sculptural fragments from Clonmacnoise. *J Roy Soc Antiq Ir*, 114 (1984), 57–62.

Edwards, N. 1990 *The Archaeology of Early Medieval Ireland*. London.

Fanning, T. and Ó hÉailidhe, P. 1980 Some cross-inscribed slabs from the Irish midlands. In Murtagh, 5–23.

Harbison, P. 1980 A lost Crucifixion plaque of Clonmacnoise type found in County Mayo. In Murtagh, 24–38.

Harbison, P. 1992 *The High Crosses of Ireland, An Iconographical and Photographic Survey*, 3 vols (*=RGZM Forschungsinstitut für Vor- und Frügeschichte, Monog 17*). Bonn.

Harbison, P 1993 A high cross base from the Rock of Cashel and a historical reconsideration of the 'Ahenny group' of crosses. *Proc Roy Ir Acad*, 93C (1993), 1–20.

Henry, F. 1967 *Irish Art during the Viking Invasions (800–1020 AD)*. London.

Hicks, C. 1980 A Clonmacnoise workshop in stone. *J Roy Soc Antiq Ir*, 110 (1980) 5–35.

Hughes, K. 1966 *The Church in Early Irish Society*. London.

Kendrick, T. D. 1939 Gallen Priory excavations, 1934–5. *J Roy Soc Antiq Ir*, 49 (1939), 1–20.

Kenney, J. F. 1929 *The sources for the early history of Ireland: Ecclesiastical, an introduction and guide*. New York (rev edn Shannon, 1968).

King, H. 1992a Excavations at Clonmacnoise. *Archaeology Ireland*, 6, 3 (1992) 12–14.

King, H. 1992b Moving crosses. *Archaeology Ireland*, 6, 4 (1992), 22–3.

Lasko, P. 1972 *Ars Sacra 800–1200*. Harmondsworth.

Leask, H. G. (n.d.) *Glendalough Co. Wicklow. Official Historical and Descriptive Guide*. Dublin.

Lionard, P. 1961 Early Irish grave-slabs. *Proc Roy Ir Acad*, 61C (1960–61), 95–169.

Macalister, R. A. S. 1909 *The memorial slabs of Clonmacnoise, King's County*. Dublin.

Macalister, R. A. S. 1916 The history and antiquities of Inis Cealtra. *Proc Roy Ir Acad*, 33C (1916), 93–174.

Macalister, R. A. S. 1921 *The Latin and Irish Lives of St Ciarán*. London.

Macdonald, A. 1981 Notes on monastic archaeology and the Annals of Ulster, 650–1050. In Ó Corráin, D. (ed.), *Irish Antiquity, Essays and Studies Presented to Professor M.J. O'Kelly*, 304–19. Cork.

Manning, C. and Moore, F. 1991 An ogham stone find from Clonmacnoise. *Archaeology Ireland*, 5, 4 (1991), 10–11.

Meyer, K. (ed.) 1901 Baile in Scáil. *Zeitschrift für celtische Philologie*, 3 (1901), 475–66.

Meyer, K. 1918 Das Ende von Baile in Scáil. *Zeitschrift für celtische Philologie*, 12 (1918), 232–8.

MIA=Ó hInnse, S. (ed. & trans.) 1947 *Miscellaneous Irish Annals (A.D. 1114–1437)*. Dublin.

Murtagh, H. (ed.) 1980 *Irish Midland Studies, Essays in Commemoration of N.W. English*. Athlone.

Mytum, H. 1992 *The origins of Early Christian Ireland*. London/New York.

Ó Carragáin, É. 1994 '*Traditio evangeliorum*' and '*sustentatio*': the relevance of liturgical ceremonies to the Book of Kells. In O'Mahony, F. (ed.), *The Book of Kells, Proceedings of a Conference at Trinity College Dublin, 6–9 September 1992*, 398–436. Aldershot.

O'Donovan, J. 1857 The Registry of Clonmacnoise; with notes and introductory remarks. *J Roy Soc Antiq Ir*, 4 (1856–57), 444–60.

Ó Floinn, R. 1997 Innovation and conservatism in Irish metalwork of the Romanesque period. In Karkov, C. Farrell, R.T. and Ryan, M. (eds), *The Insular Tradition* (=*American Early Medieval Stud* 3), 259–81. Oxford, Ohio.

Ó hÉailidhe, P. 1967 The crosses and slabs at St Berrihert's Kyle, in the Glen of Aherlow. In Rynne, E. (ed.), *North Munster Studies, Essays in Commemoration of Monsignor Michael Moloney*, 103–26. Limerick.

Ó Keefe, T. 1995 The Romanesque portal at Clonfert Cathedral and its iconography. In Bourke, C. (ed.), *From the Isles of the North: Early Medieval Art in Ireland and Britain*, 261–69. Belfast.

Ó Murchadha, D. 1980 Rubbings taken of the inscriptions on the Cross of the Scriptures, Clonmacnoise. *J Roy Soc Antiq Ir*, 110 (1980), 47–51.

Ó Murchadha, D. and Ó Murchú, G. 1988 Fragmentary inscriptions from the west cross at Durrow, the south cross at Clonmacnois, and the cross of Kinnitty. *J Roy Soc Antiq Ir*, 118 (1988), 53–66.

Petrie, G. 1845 *The Ecclesiastical Architecture of Ireland*. Dublin.

Petrie, G. 1872 *Christian Inscriptions in the Irish Language. Chiefly Collected and Drawn by George Petrie, LL.D.* (Stokes, M. (ed)), vol. I. Dublin.

Ryan, J. 1973 *Clonmacnois—A Historical Summary*. Dublin.

Ryan, M. (ed.) 1983 *Treasures of Ireland, Irish Art 3000 B.C.—1500 A.D.* Dublin.

Stokes, W. (ed. & trans.) 1905 *Félire Óengusso Céli Dé, The Martyrology of Oengus the Culdee* (=*Henry Bradshaw Soc* 29). London.

Swarzenski, H. 1967 *Monuments of Romanesque Art* (2nd edn). Chicago.

Waddell, J. and Holland, P. 1990 The Peakaun site: Duignan's 1944 investigations. *Tipperary Hist J* (1990), 165–86.

9. A GROUP OF SHAFTS AND RELATED SCULPTURE FROM CLONMACNOISE AND ITS ENVIRONS

Nancy Edwards

Clonmacnoise has by far the largest collection of early medieval stone sculpture from anywhere in Ireland. The best-known pieces are the so-called 'Cross of the Scriptures' and the South Cross (Harbison 1992, i, nos 54, 56; Edwards 1986), but there is also a closely comparable group of shafts and related sculpture: the North Shaft and two other small shafts from Clonmacnoise (nos II and III), the shaft from Banagher and the cross from Bealin (Harbison 1992, i, nos 55, 58–9, 20, 22). In addition there is a small twelfth-century cross fragment decorated with a pair of confronted interlocking lions (Harbison 1992, no. 57; Edwards 1984, 59–60) and a variety of Hiberno-Romanesque architectural carving on Temple Finghin and the Nuns' Church (Manning 1994a, 30–3). However, by far the most numerous monuments are the graveslabs, of which almost 700, whole or fragmentary, have now been recorded (Petrie 1872; Macalister 1909; 1949; Lionard 1961). Together the carvings testify to the existence of an important sculptural workshop at Clonmacnoise, which, though it may not have been working continually, perhaps spanned the eighth to the late twelfth centuries.

This study is concerned with the group of shafts from Clonmacnoise and Banagher and the cross at Bealin (Ills 1–17). These monuments have been considered in the past, most notably by Henry (1965, 143–7), Hicks (1980) and Harbison (1992, i, 377–9), but they have not received the more detailed attention they deserve largely because they are decorated predominantly with Insular ornament. Although there are some figural and animal representations, there is no Scriptural iconography.

Location

The recent excavation around the base of the North Shaft (Manning 1992) prior to removing it into the visitor centre indicated that it was not *in situ*. On Jonas Blaymires's 1739 plan of Clonmacnoise it is shown in the same position, to the north of the Cathedral, but surrounded by a walled enclosure labelled as the burial-place of the Malones (Manning 1994b, 20). According to records in the National Museum, Clonmacnoise II (Inv. no. 1929: 1494–6) was brought to the museum from Clonmacnoise in 1929. Clonmacnoise III, also now in the visitor centre, was first mentioned in 1896–7 (Allen 1896–7, 312) and in 1909 it was located in Temple Dowling (Macalister 1909, 154). It was broken in two more than 30 years ago (Harbison 1992, i, 57). The cross now located on Twyford demesne at Bealin some ten miles to the north-east of Clonmacnoise is almost certainly not in its original position (Harbison 1992, i, 26). Henry (1965, 143) suggested that it might originally have been the East Cross marked on both James Ware's 1658 and Blaymires's 1739 engravings of Clonmacnoise (Manning 1994b, 18, 20), but this cannot be proved. It is more likely that the cross comes from Twyford itself, where it has been suggested (Anon. 1951) that *Iseal Chiaráin*, the site of what seems to have been a Culdee hermitage connected with Clonmacnoise (O'Donovan 1856, AD 1031, 1072), was located. The Banagher shaft, which was also brought from Clonmacnoise to the National Museum in 1929, is known to have once stood by the spring in the Market Square adjacent to the churchyard at Banagher (Cooke 1853, 277–80), approximately twelve miles down the Shannon, though it is unclear whether this siting was original. But despite the fact that this group of monuments is likely to come from three different sites, the carving indicates that they are clearly associated and are all the products of sculptors connected with Clonmacnoise.

Left: Ill. 1—Clonmacnoise North Shaft Face A. Centre: Ill. 2—Clonmacnoise North Shaft Face B. Right: Ill. 3—Clonmacnoise North Shaft Face D.

Stone

In the early medieval period local stone was favoured for sculpture because of the difficulties of transportation. Therefore it is interesting that amongst these monuments two different types of stone are used. Bealin, the North Shaft and Clonmacnoise II are of limestone; this is the local stone, but it has weathered badly. In contrast, the base of the North Shaft is of sandstone conglomerate and could originally have functioned as a millstone (Manning 1992). However, Banagher and Clonmacnoise III, as well as all the other crosses and graveslabs from Clonmacnoise, are of superior-quality sandstone. The nearest outcrop of sandstone is some miles from Clonmacnoise (Geological Survey, sheet 108), and Lionard (1961, 145) suggested that the stone might have been transported up the Shannon from as far away as south Clare, an interesting theory which would certainly be worth testing with the aid of petrological analysis. At any rate, the variation in stone suggests experimentation and a conscious effort to find better stone for carving. A parallel for this is found at Iona, where St Oran's Cross is carved from a schist susceptible to lamination from the Ross of Mull nearby, but the two largest pieces of St John's Cross are carved from high-quality schist imported from Mid-Argyll, whereas the smaller components are also of Ross of Mull schist; St Martin's Cross is carved from grey epidiorite, probably also from the Argyll mainland (RCAHMS 1982, 17, 192, 201, 205).

Left: Ill. 4—Clonmacnoise II Face A.   Centre: Ill. 5—Clonmacnoise II Face B. Right: Ill. 6—Clonmacnoise
II Face D.

Left: Ill. 7—Clonmacnoise III Face A. Centre: Ill. 8—Clonmacnoise III Face B. Right:
Ill. 9—Clonmacnoise III Face D.

From left to right: Ill. 10—Banagher Face A. Ill. 11—Banagher Face B. Ill. 12—Banagher Face C. Ill. 13—Banagher Face D.

The form of the monuments

A variety of monument types are represented within the group and may be indicative of experimentation with a variety of free-standing sculptural types. Such experimentation is also clearly apparent at Iona, where a number of cross types are found (RCAHMS 1982, 17–18). The North Shaft is clearly no longer complete since it has a tenon projecting from the top. This could have supported a cross head without a ring, a suggestion made more likely by the recent excavation of the base, which indicates that the monument was intended to be free-standing despite the fact that Face C is uncarved. For this reason Henry's (1965, 144) suggestion that it might form one vertical side of a rectangular door frame is now untenable (Bourke 1986, 116). As Manning (1992) has noted, the complex, circular stepped base, which has four vertical grooves corresponding with the corners of the shaft, may have been adapted from a millstone and may once have been encased in a stone box in a similar manner to the base of St John's Cross, Iona, which also makes use of an adapted millstone (RCAHMS 1982, 213–15). The original form of the Banagher shaft is unclear, though it is evident that it was intended to be free-standing since it is carved on all four faces. There is a small mortice hole in the centre of the top of the shaft, but this is hardly large enough to support a superstructure of any size. The shaft has definitely been the subject of secondary alteration since a rectangular slot has been cut into the top of both narrow faces straight through the carving. It might have been carried out to facilitate the insertion of a composite ring for a cross head, but this is impossible to prove. Clonmacnoise II and III, which have very similar dimensions, are only carved on three faces. They were clearly designed to stand upright; Clonmacnoise II has a tenon at the bottom which presumably fitted into a base, but the top of the shaft is now damaged. Their original

Ill. 14—Bealin Face A.

Ill. 15—Bealin Face B.

Ill. 16—Bealin Face C.

Ill. 17—Bealin Face D.

functions are unknown, though Clonmacnoise III cannot have been part of a free-standing cross.

Bealin is the only definite cross within the group. The cross head type is the same as the South Cross, Clonmacnoise, and is also paralleled elsewhere in Ireland (Edwards 1986, 24). But, interestingly, it is much more common in Pictland and Dalriada, for example on the Class II Pictish slab Aberlemno 2 (Allen and Anderson 1903, iii, fig. 227A) and St Martin's Cross, Iona, though the latter also has slots on the ends of the horizontal cross arms to enable the addition of wood or metal extensions (RCAHMS 1982, 204–5). The placement of the bosses on Face A of the cross head at Bealin is also comparable with Clonmacnoise South as well as the Ahenny crosses and Kilree (Edwards 1986, 24). The Bealin cross head appears large and heavy compared with the size of the shaft, though, if the cross ever had a base, this would have made the proportions more even. The layout of the ornament on Face C, especially the triquetra knot occupying a rectangular space on the upper cross arm, seems rather clumsy—a series of unconnected motifs rather than an overall design. Again this might suggest experimentation, where the sculptor may have been trying to adapt Insular ornamental motifs to an unfamiliar sculptural form.

The carving

Hicks (1980, 7–12) suggested that the most characteristic features of the group were animals, lions in particular, which were placed singly or in vertical rows. Although such animals are one feature of the decoration, it is Insular ornament, particularly interlace, but also zoomorphic and anthropomorphic designs, and to a lesser extent spirals and chequerboards, which dominates these monuments.

Interlace

Interlace is used extensively on all the monuments in this group and the repertoire of patterns and methods of construction are closely comparable; they are also paralleled on Clonmacnoise South (Edwards 1986, 28–9, fig. 2.3). As I have shown elsewhere (Edwards 1983a, 13–16), the interlace patterns were generally constructed on a horizontal/vertical grid of squares, and these monuments are linked by the use of certain unit measures in the construction of the grids, particularly 3cm. The group is also bound together by the use of a similar repertoire of interlace patterns (Ill. 18) and, even though some of the ornament is severely weathered, it is frequently possible to reconstruct the patterns as, for example, on the North Shaft, Face A (Ills 1 and 18g, j, k, b, r), where, apart from the third panel down, the interlace strands are organised so as to leave cruciform voids in the centres, thereby forming negative cross symbols (Stevenson 1981–2, 20). This group of monuments exhibits the greatest variety of interlace patterns found on any group of crosses in Ireland. Nevertheless the repertoire is surprisingly small. A variety of strand types are also used: a rounded strand in fairly low relief is the most common, but double strands (e.g. Ill. 18x), strands with median lines or grooves (e.g. Ill. 14, top of shaft) and one example of a humped strand on Clonmacnoise III Face D (Ill. 9) are also found. The variations in appearance are well demonstrated on Bealin. The lace-like character of the panel on Face A of the shaft (Ill. 18r), Encircled and Turned E (Cramp 1984, xxviii–xlv), is achieved using a small unit measure, 1.5cm, and a slender strand width, 0.75cm. This contrasts with the much heavier plaitwork above (Ills 14 and 18v), which has a unit measure of 6cm and a bulky strand consisting of two strands set side by side with a median groove, together 3.5cm wide. In fact three distinctive styles may be recognised amongst the group. First, Bealin, Banagher and the North Shaft all make use of large-scale patterns, including examples where a single pattern element is enlarged to decorate an entire panel as, for example, the panel at the end of the cross arm on Bealin Face B, which is carved with a single unit of Half B with bar terminals

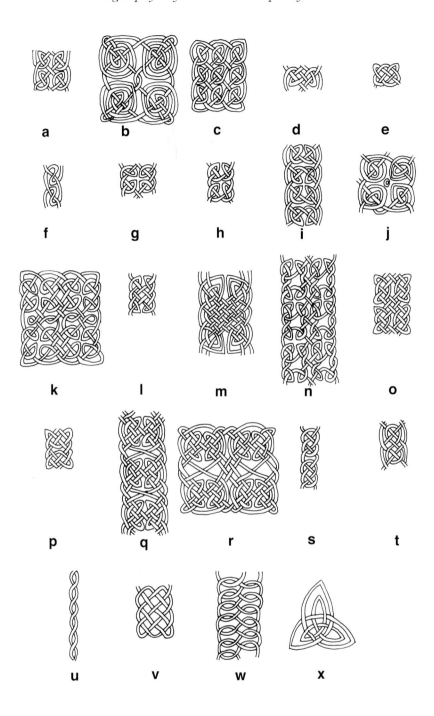

*Ill. 18—Interlace ornament: **a** Basic A, Bealin Face D; **b** Spiralled and Surrounded A, North Shaft Face A;*
*c Basic A three elements abreast, Banagher Face C; **d** Basic B (adaptation), Clonmacnoise III Face B; **e***
*Turned B, North Shaft Face B, Clonmacnoise III Face B; **f** Half-B, Bealin Face B; **g** Basic C, Bealin Face*
*A; as a roundel, Bealin Face A, North Shaft Face A; **h** Turned C, North Shaft Face B, Clonmacnoise II Face*
*B, Clonmacnoise III Face B; **i** Turned C with outside strands, Banagher Face D; **j** Spiralled and Surrounded*
*C, North Shaft Face A; **k** Basic C four elements abreast, North Shaft Face A; **l** Turned D, Clonmacnoise III*
*Face B; **m** Turned D with double strands, Banagher Face C; **n** Variation of Turned D four elements abreast,*
*Banagher Face B; **o** Basic E, Bealin Face B; **p** Turned E, Clonmacnoise II Face D; **q** Encircled and Turned*
*E, Banagher Face D; **r** Encircled and Turned E, North Shaft Face A, Bealin Face A; **s** Simple F, Banagher*
*Face A, Bealin Face A; **t** Closed Circuit F with outside strands, Clonmacnoise III Face B; **u** Two-strand plait,*
*Bealin Face A; **v** Six-strand plait, North Shaft Face B, Clonmacnoise II Face D, Clonmacnoise III Face B, Bealin*
*Face A; **w** Interlocking pattern, Banagher Face B, Bealin Face D; **x** Double Triquetra knot, Bealin Face C.*

Ill. 19—Clonmacnoise II Faces B and D, showing reconstructions of changing interlace patterns.

at the top and bottom (Ill. 17). The thick strands are broken up by the use of a median line or groove or by doubling the strand. Secondly, there is a distinctive, delicate lace-like style using complex patterns, typified by the panels on the North Shaft Face A, but also found on the shaft of Bealin Face A and at the bottom of the shaft on Banagher Face D, where the loose strands terminate in birds' heads which grasp further strands in their beaks (Ill. 18q). Thirdly, six- or eight-strand patterns are used to decorate long, narrow panels, the monotony being broken by the use of changing patterns, typified by Clonmacnoise II (Ill. 19). Similar patterns are also found on Banagher Face D and Clonmacnoise II (Edwards 1984, 58), though, in the case of Banagher, the patterns (Ill. 18q, i) have ten or more strands and are therefore planned on a very small scale in order to fit them into the available space.

The delicate style of many of the patterns on these monuments, for example the North Shaft Face A, is undoubtedly reminiscent of the manuscript medium. Close comparisons are difficult, but some general parallels may be drawn with the Book of Kells (Dublin, Trinity Coll. Lib. MS A.1.6). Many of the simpler Clonmacnoise patterns are also found in the Book of Kells. For example, the trick of adapting Basic C elements to form a roundel is closely paralleled on f. 2^v, and on f. 5^r the Basic C pattern is surrounded by an outer band of interlace almost identical to the roundel on the cross head of Bealin Face A. Henry (1974, 205) describes the interlace in the Book of Kells as the 'stock in trade of Insular illumination and lacking in any great virtuosity', and this is also true of many of the simpler patterns on the Clonmacnoise monuments. On the whole the Clonmacnoise interlace is not reminiscent of metalworking techniques, but comparisons can be made with sheet-metal objects engraved with interlace as, for example, the *Domnach Airgid* (Raftery 1941, pl. 117), where the choice of pattern and the fineness of line are both reminiscent of the delicate interlace on Bealin and the North Shaft.

Zoomorphic and anthropomorphic motifs

Confronted dragonesque beasts with interlocking beaks. A great variety of dragonesque beast motifs are found in the repertoire of Insular ornament (Edwards 1990, 54–5). However, the confronted dragonesque beasts with interlocking beaks on Bealin Face A (Ill. 20a), where they are used to decorate the awkward space around the low boss at the top of the shaft, are unusual. The one close parallel for the Bealin motif is provided by a small, domed gilt-bronze mount now in the National Museum of Copenhagen (Ill. 20b), which Wilson (1955) has suggested could be Irish and late eighth-century. However, the beasts on this mount lack paws because the tops of their bodies are hidden. They also lack eyes, but there is a suggestion of a curved ear, though this does not project as on Bealin. A second, less close comparison may be made with the two beasts cast in high relief which form finials on the ridge-pole of a house-shrine in the National Museum, Dublin (Mahr 1932, pl. 18.1). Each beast has small paws and a long open beak. The two beasts confront each other on either side of a human face mask set at the centre of the ridge-piece. The general background to the evolution of this motif can be seen in Germanic animal ornament as, for example, on the Benty Grange mount (Henry 1965, fig. 20a) or in the Book of Durrow on the St John carpet-page (Dublin, Trinity Coll. Lib. MS A.4.5, f. 192^v; Alexander 1978, pl. 22).

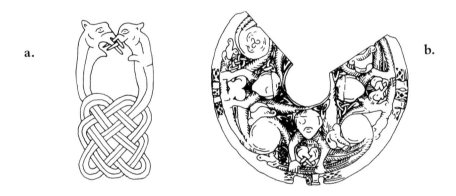

*Ill. 20—Confronted dragonesque beasts with interlocking beaks: **a** Bealin Face A; **b** Copenhagen Mount (after Wilson 1995).*

Serpents with interlaced bodies. At the bottom of Bealin Face D there is an unusual interlocking figure-of-eight interlace pattern which is designed so as to use only one strand (Ill. 18w). The upper end terminates in a snake's head, the lower in a slashed fish tail. There is a much less elegant version of what is almost certainly the same motif on Banagher Face B at the top of the shaft, though the serpent's head is now missing. This is not the well-known serpent of Pictish and Dalriadic 'Boss Style' sculpture (Henderson 1987) and high-relief Insular metalwork (e.g. Mahr 1932, pl. 32.1). Much better parallels are instead provided by the more delicate filigree snakes on objects such as the Hunterston and 'Tara' brooches (Stevenson 1974, 24, pls XVI–XVII; Whitfield 1993, fig. 14.16). In Pictish sculpture there is also a more delicate serpent and this perhaps provides the best parallel for the Clonmacnoise monuments. These serpents, or similar beasts with fish tails, appear on several of the Pictish stones which show a preference for monsters, for example Meigle 4 (Allen and Anderson 1903, iii, fig. 313B). In Ireland there are similar serpents on the North Cross at Duleek (Harbison 1992, ii, figs 242, 244).

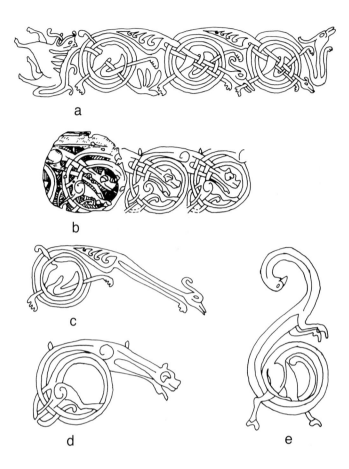

*Ill. 21—Birds and animals with spiralled bodies: **a** Bealin Face C (after Crawford 1980); **b** Torshov Mount (after Bakka 1965); **c** Bealin, detail; **d** Torshov Mount, detail; **e** Aberlemno 2, detail.*

Birds and animals with spiralled bodies. On Bealin Face C a procession of three birds with spiralled bodies spans almost the entire length of the shaft (Ill. 21a). This is a large-scale motif used in an unusual way, but the low flat relief gives it a delicate appearance. There is a similar procession at the bottom of Banagher Face B, where the birds have been carved on a very small scale and are therefore so squashed as to be almost unrecognisable. There are also comparable motifs on the North Shaft. First, the second panel down on Face D has a simple but nevertheless related motif where all the diagonals and appendages have been left out, leaving a single vertical 'S' scroll terminating in the centre of each spiral with a bird's head. There is a similar bird's-head spiral terminal on Kilree (Harbison 1992, ii, fig. 449). Secondly, on Face B there is a pair of confronted beasts with spiralled bodies.

The origins of processions of birds and animals with spiralled bodies probably goes back to imported Eastern Mediterranean manuscripts and textiles, but the motif was honed to Insular taste and can be seen, for example, in the Lindisfarne Gospels f. 26^V (London, B.L. MS Cotton Nero D.IV; Bruce-Mitford 1960, 253). The 'S' scrolls with bird's-head terminals on this page provide a good if early parallel for the bird's-head spiral motif on the North Shaft Face D. However, the best parallels for the Bealin procession are to be found on a group of Insular sheet-metal objects decorated with engraved designs which have mainly come to light in Viking graves in Norway. The closest parallel is provided by a fragmentary piece of bronze sheet from Torshov (Wamers 1985, no. 138) (Ill. 21b). Although a quadruped is shown, the layout of the design is almost identical to the Bealin birds (Ill. 21c, d). Processions of birds and animals with spiralled bodies are also frequently found in the Book of Kells, as, for example, on f. 32^v where each creature, instead of stretching over two spiral units as on Bealin, forms a single unit, its head and front leg forming the diagonals to the body spiral of the same animal. On f. 200^r there is a complex procession of birds and quadrupeds where each creature stretches over two registers of the pattern, the head and neck forming the diagonals of the first unit, the body coiling into the second to form a letter, and a bird is also intermeshed in the letter form (Henry 1974, pls 26 and 63). There are also some interesting parallels with Pictish early Class II slabs, notably a large-scale bird motif on Aberlemno 2 (Allen and Anderson 1903, iii, fig. 227A). The Aberlemno motif is placed vertically and planned on a large scale comparable with Bealin, though the style of carving is less delicate. Like the motif on the North Shaft Face D, each bird, which bites at the body of the bird above, is formed from an 'S' scroll (Ill. 21e) and, like Bealin, each bird stretches over two spiral units with the lower end of each spiral terminating in a hip and two feet, but each bird has four limbs rather than three as on Bealin.

Anthropomorphic motifs.

There are two examples of anthropomorphic ornament on Banagher and two on the North Shaft. On Banagher Face C two confronted men are shown emerging from interlace; the loose strands of their interlaced forelocks are caught in the clenched fists of the right-hand man; the man on the left holds the other by the wrists. The panel on Banagher Face A is broken at the bottom but originally showed four men set diagonally, with their legs, one flexed and one extended, interlaced in the centre of the panel, forming a negative cross. They face right and have long beards and hair, the strands of which curl round their wrists and are then grasped in the hands of adjacent figures. As Bourke (1986, 117–19, fig. 13) recognised, a fragmentary motif at the top of the North Shaft Face B shows the legs of a man, one flexed and one extended, interlaced with the body of a snake which terminates in a fish tail. On Face D of the North Shaft the man sitting cross-legged with tendrils of hair and a mask-like face is not Cernunnus, a pagan antlered god, as has often been suggested (Henry 1965, 155; Ross 1967, 147), but rather a decorative anthropomorphic motif like the rest (Hicks 1980, 20–1).

The best comparisons for such motifs are to be found in Insular manuscripts and especially in the Book of Kells, where countless figures have been incorporated into the ornament (Hicks 1980, 19–22; Bourke 1986, 119–20). The use of men's heads as interlace terminals may be seen on f. 33^r (Henry 1974, pl. 108). The figures in the canon-tables (e.g. f. 1^v, f. 2^r, f. 3^v) may be closely compared with both the Banagher panels as they too have elongated bodies, flat tops to their heads, and frequently long hair, beards and forelocks which extend into interlace strands which they clutch in their fists. Like Banagher Face A and the North Shaft Face C, their long thin legs are frequently flexed rather than extended. For the most part these figures are interlaced with delicate tendrils rather than with one another, but in other contexts (e.g. f. 34^r, f. 130^r, f. 253^v) there are complete anthropomorphic figures with their limbs, forelocks and beards interlaced. Other less-accomplished manuscript parallels include examples in the Book of MacRegol (Oxford, Bodleian Lib. MS Auct. D.2.19, f. 52; Alexander 1978, pl. 267) and the Turin Gospels (Turin, Bibl. Nazionale, Cod. 0.IV.20, f. 129; Alexander 1978, pl. 278).

Examples of anthropomorphic motifs on Pictish sculpture are concentrated at Meigle and, like those on Banagher and the North Shaft, share some close similarities with the Book of Kells (Henderson 1982, 94–6, pls IXb, Xb, XIIb, d). On Meigle 11 the figure grasping two serpents and on Meigle 22 a figure with strands of interlaced hair whose body rises out of interlace which terminates in two fish tails (Allen and Anderson 1903, iii, fig. 350) may both be compared with the motifs on the North Shaft. There are also examples of anthropomorphic designs elsewhere on Irish sculpture, on Ahenny North, the South and Market Crosses at Kells, Monasterboice South and the 'Cross of the Scriptures' at Clonmacnoise (Harbison 1992, ii, fig. 533; iii, figs 1031–5), but their stylistic affinities are on the whole less close to those on Banagher and the North Shaft than the parallels with manuscript illumination.

Anthropomorphic motifs are not very common in metalwork. However, an Insular gilt-bronze mount found at Halsan in Norway (Bakka 1965, 39, figs 4–6) and the filigree panels on the Derrynaflan paten (Ryan 1983, 19, c. pl. 11) have several stylistic similarities with the Banagher panels. The Oseburg bucket escutcheon provides a good parallel for the cross-legged figure on the North Shaft (Henry 1965, pl. 91).

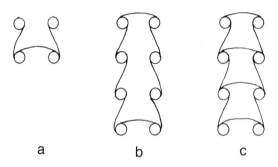

*Ill. 22—Spiral patterns: **a** Bealin Face D; **b** Clonmacnoise II Face A; **c** Banagher Faces B and D.*

Spirals

Spiral patterns, although not extensively used on the Clonmacnoise monuments, are nevertheless characteristic, being found on Bealin, Banagher and Clonmacnoise II (Ill. 22); the only spirals on the North Shaft are the 'S' scroll with bird's-head terminals on Face D and incidental ornament on the anthropomorphic motif on Face B. The spiral patterns on Bealin Face D and Clonmacnoise II Face A may be closely compared; those on Banagher Faces B and D have similar patterns of 'S' scrolls linked horizontally by 'C' scrolls but they are on a much smaller scale. The striking feature about these spiral patterns is the detail of vegetal ornament. In each case the 'S' scroll expansions are leaf-shaped. On Clonmacnoise II the spiral terminals have details reminiscent of berry bunches, and the remaining 'C' scroll expansion, with its funnel-shaped slashes and round knob hanging down from the centre, has a flower-like quality. At the bottom of the panel there are small projections reminiscent of the point where a plant stalk issues from the earth. I have argued elsewhere (1984, 57–8) that these plant elements could be interpreted as a method by which Insular artists absorbed vine scroll, with all its symbolic connotations, into a Celtic ornamental repertoire.

Step patterns

Step patterns do not form a major part of the ornament on these monuments. In fact there are only two examples: on Bealin Face B and Clonmacnoise II Face B (Ill. 23). Neither are prominently placed. The origins of step patterns clearly lie in metalwork (Edwards 1983b, 19–20), and the Emly house-shrine (Swarzenski 1954), where the lines of the step pattern have first been cut out of the wood and then silver hammered into them so that it

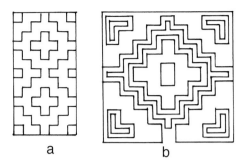

Ill. 23—Step patterns: **a** *Clonmacnoise II Face B;* **b** *Bealin Face B.*

protrudes, giving a contrast between the shining silver and the dark wood, provides a particularly good parallel for the Bealin motif, which, when viewed in oblique lighting, gives a very similar effect. Step patterns are also found on the Ossory crosses (Edwards 1983b, 19–20) but are most characteristic of those at Kilree and Killamery (Edwards 1990, 47–9).

Lions, griffins and other fantastic beasts
The lion at the top of Banagher Face A is shown in profile facing right, its left legs raised in motion. Its large head has a pointed ear, large almond-shaped eye, rather square jaws outlined by an incised line, and a lolling tongue. Its snout terminates in a rounded knob. It has prominent paws, a floriate tail with leaf-shaped tufts which arches over its back, and there are traces of a curly mane at the base of the spine. There are similar lions at the bottom of the shaft on Bealin Face C and on the North Shaft Face D. On Banagher Face C there is also a second lion with a tail and a lolling tongue which extend into interlace strands. But there are also two slightly different animals: one on the cross head of Bealin Face C, the second immediately below the anthropomorphic motif on Face D of the North Shaft. Hicks (1980, 9–11) suggested that these were also lions, but they appear to have beaks rather than elongated jaws and for this reason may be identified as wingless griffins. On Clonmacnoise III Face A there are three similar but less well-executed quadrupeds; therefore it is difficult to tell whether lions or griffins are intended.

Both the lion and the griffin were imbued with Christian symbolism. The lion is chiefly seen as a symbol of strength. Amongst other meanings, the early Christian fathers sometimes associated it with Christ; in Byzantine theological writings it was seen as the sign of the Resurrection, and in the early bestiary known as the *Physiologus* it symbolised the Incarnation (Cabrol and Leclercq 1907–53, IX.1, 1198–9). The lion is also associated with St Mark, but this is unlikely here since no other Evangelist symbols are represented. The Christian significance of the griffin, which also appears in the *Physiologus*, has recently been studied by Ryan (1993, 156–60), who has emphasised its apotropaic character as well as its associations with Eucharistic iconography.

Hicks (1980, 11–12) has commented upon the manuscript parallels for the Clonmacnoise lions, suggesting that the Evangelist symbol in the Book of Durrow (f. 191^{V}; Alexander 1978, pl. 16) may have provided a model, but such a direct comparison seems unnecessary. The lion, though not the griffin, is also a characteristic ornamental element in the Book of Kells (Henry 1974, 206–7). These lions (e.g. f. 3^{r}, f. 187^{V}, f. 212^{r}), though considerably more elegant, with their pointed ears, large almond-shaped eyes, spiralled snouts and curly manes, have many features in common with those on the Clonmacnoise-group monuments. In metalwork stylised wingless griffins constructed out of filigree have been identified on the Derrynaflan chalice (Ryan 1993, 151).

Lions and griffins are both found on sculpture elsewhere. In Ireland, for example, there are two lions on the large slab at Gallen Priory, on the Tybroughney pillar and the cross at Moone (Harbison 1992, i, nos 181, 224; ii, figs 516, 627–8), and there is a wingless griffin on the Roscrea pillar (Harbison 1992, i, no. 195; ii, fig. 548). On Pictish monuments there are lions on Papil and Golspie, and the curious shape of the lion's feet on Glamis 2, a distinctive feature of Pictish animal representations, is also found on the lion and griffin on Bealin (Allen and Anderson 1903, iii, figs 6, 48B, 234A). In Pictland the griffin is also quite commonly shown, particularly on monuments from Meigle and St Vigeans. There is a particularly lively example of a wingless griffin on Meigle 26 (Allen and Anderson 1903, iii, fig. 318C). Cramp (1978, 13) has discussed the influence of exotic oriental beasts on the sculptural repertoire of Anglo-Saxon England during the last quarter of the eighth and first quarter of the ninth century, and has suggested (1978, 8) that this influx was due to the re-establishment of Orthodoxy by the Empress Irene. Lions and griffins became popular motifs on both Northumbrian and Mercian sculpture. The types may be exemplified by the prancing lions at Breedon (Cramp 1977, 206–7), the classical winged lion entangled in a vine on Dacre 1 (Bailey and Cramp 1988, 90–1, ill. 239), and the griffins at Otley (Cramp 1978, fig. 1.2). It seems likely that the lions and griffins on the Clonmacnoise monuments are the products of similar orientalising influences. Models may well have reached Ireland directly from the East, perhaps in the form of textiles. Other possible models include portraits in bestiaries. Lions and griffins are also found on both sculpture and buckles in Merovingian Gaul (Ryan 1993, 156–8).

Below the griffin on the North Shaft Face B is a backward-looking bird with four legs and hooves. This cannot be identified as any particular mythical species but is comparable with other fantastic beasts found on the Roscrea and Tybroughney pillars (Harbison 1992, i, nos 195, 224). The models for such animals are likely to have been derived from illustrated bestiaries where the beasts are characterised by attitudes and associations which are given a Christian symbolic meaning. The *Physiologus* was an early and popular example of this genre. Versions of the bestiary were available in both Ireland and Anglo-Saxon England at an early date: for example, Bede knew of a work entitled *De naturis bestiarum*. But unfortunately no early manuscripts from Britain and Ireland have survived (Allen and Anderson 1903, i, xi–xlvi). Another work on which the bestiary drew and which could have provided suitable models is Isidore of Seville's *Etymologiae*. This compilation, which is concerned with gathering together secular knowledge (Bréhaut 1912, 30), includes a section on beasts both natural and mythical. However, unlike the *Physiologus*, Isidore does not seek to draw moral or spiritual lessons from them (Bréhaut 1912, 222–3). The works of Isidore of Seville were available in Ireland as early as the second half of the seventh century (Hillgarth 1961–2, 185–9).

Horsemen and hunting scenes
The only securely identifiable hunting scene is on Bealin. It is inconspicuously placed in an unusual position for Irish sculptural hunting scenes at the bottom of the shaft on Face B. It consists of a stag with two branched antlers and a lolling tongue shown in profile facing right, its right hind leg gripped in the jaws of a hound, which is shown in profile facing left and placed beneath. Below again is a long-haired horseman with a spear resting on his right shoulder shown in profile facing right. A triquetra knot fills the space between the spearhead and the horse's body. Hunting scenes are common on the Irish crosses, but the only good parallel for the scene on Bealin is on the left cross arm of Dromiskin, where a stag is shown being chased by a hound and followed by a horseman (Harbison 1992, i, no. 77; ii, fig. 209), this time placed horizontally rather than vertically. As Henry (1965, 143) has pointed out,

the composition of the Bealin panel has much in common with hunting scenes on the Class II Pictish slabs, for example Hilton of Cadboll, Elgin, Burghead 7 and Meigle 12 (Allen and Anderson 1903, iii, figs 59, 137–8, 346C). It is likely that such scenes were common because of the popularity of hunting as an aristocratic pastime, but in this context a religious meaning would also have been appropriate: possibly the stag signified Christ crucified and the hounds evil, thus representing Christ's redemptive sacrifice (Bailey 1977, 68–71). A similar symbolism may apply to the stag shown on Banagher Face A, its foreleg caught in a trap (Gillespie 1918–19, 165–7). In this context it is interesting to note the wording of Psalm 90, v. 3, where the psalmist pleads to be freed from the 'snare' (*laqueo*) of the huntsman. Traps similar to that shown are to be found in the National Museum, where they have been identified as deer-traps.

Above the stag on Banagher Face A is an ecclesiastic on horseback; his right arm catches up the folds of his garment and a crozier is shown resting on his left shoulder. This jaunty figure finds its closest comparisons with intertextual illustrations on f. 89^r and f. 255^v in the Book of Kells (Henry 1974, pls 76, 121). Horsemen, who might be identified as ecclesiastics, are also found on Pictish sculpture, for example Dunfallandy (Allen and Anderson 1903, iii, fig. 305B). The horseman on Clonmacnoise III Face A is very similar to that on Banagher except he does not have a crozier.

The Bealin inscription

The inscription is located at the bottom of the shaft on Face A (Ill. 24). It is carved in relief in six lines and uses the half-uncial script. It reads 'OROIT DO AR TUATHGAIL LAS DERNATH IN CHROSSA', 'A prayer for Tuathgal under whose auspices this cross was made' (Macalister 1949, no. 871). Henry (1930) equated the Tuathgal mentioned in the inscription with the abbot of Clonmacnoise who died in 811 (Mac Airt and Mac Niocaill 1983, 266–7). This led her to suggest (Henry 1965, 143–4) that the cross was erected between 799, when the obit of the previous abbot is recorded (Mac Airt and Mac Niocaill 1983, 254–5), and Tuathgal's death in 811. Her argument was backed up by a study of the letter forms. A re-examination of the inscription by Kenneth Jackson (pers. comm.) suggested that palaeographically the inscription was eighth-century, though the early ninth century 'was not at all impossible', and that, although the name Tuathgal was rare, it was not unique, as Henry had supposed.

The use of relief for inscriptions is unusual, and

0   30cm

Ill. 24—Inscription, Bealin Face A (after Macalister 1949).

the Bealin inscription must have been laborious to carve. A few parallels are provided by the now-illegible inscription on Killamery (Harbison 1992, i, no. 146; ii, fig. 411), two eighth-century Anglo-Saxon graveslabs from Wensley (Okasha 1971, pls 120–1), and the Latin inscription from Tarbat in Scotland, which uses display script rather than half-uncials and may be dated to the second half of the eighth century (Higgitt 1982). In contrast, all the inscriptions on the Irish crosses with predominantly figural carving are incised. Higgitt (1982, 316–17) argued that, while relief inscriptions may have evolved independently in the British Isles, influence from Rome, where Pope John VII (705–7) is known to have had relief inscriptions carved in both Greek and Latin, is a distinct possibility.

The dating of the monuments

Although it is now impossible to prove that the Bealin inscription relates to Tuathgal the abbot of Clonmacnoise 798–811, the identification is not inherently unlikely since the art-historical comparisons would also tend to point towards a late eighth-century date.

Concerning stone sculpture, although some similarities have been noted with other Irish monuments, more significant comparisons have been made with sculpture in Scotland. These similarities were first remarked upon by Allen (1896–7, 309) and have since been discussed by Stevenson (1956, 91–3), Henry (1965, 145) and Hicks (1980, 26). First, parallels may be drawn between the Clonmacnoise group and the early Class II slabs of southern Pictland. The parallels between Bealin and Aberlemno 2, with its low relief, the shape of the cross head with its central roundel, the large-scale motifs, some of the interlace types, the preference for decorating the length of the shaft with a single pattern, the procession of birds with spiralled bodies, and the use of figural scenes with secular as well as religious connotations, are all common to both monuments (Allen and Anderson 1903, iii, figs 227A, B). The date of Class II slabs of this kind is disputed but they are generally agreed to be eighth-century, and it has been suggested that they may have been carved around the middle of the eighth century with high-relief 'Boss Style' sculpture developing by *c*. 800 (Stevenson 1955, 112–20). Indeed, as Hicks has noted (1980, 26), none of the monuments in the Clonmacnoise group have high-relief bosses, which could suggest that they were carved before the evolution of 'Boss Style'. Secondly, several interesting parallels—the use of serpents, anthropomorphic motifs, griffins and other fantastic beasts—have been suggested with a variety of sculpture from Meigle, also in southern Pictland. Similarites have also been noted with the late eighth-century Iona crosses in Dalriada, especially in their experimentation with a variety of stone and monument types, as well as the form of the base of the North Shaft and St John's Cross.

Turning to manuscripts, similarities have been noted between the Clonmacnoise monuments and elements in the repertoire and style of Insular manuscript illumination, especially the Book of Kells. Although there is still some disagreement about the date and scriptorium of the Book of Kells, many would now see it as a product of Iona in the late eighth century (Alexander 1978, 73).

Though less important, various similarities have also been mentioned with Insular metalwork objects of the late seventh to early ninth centuries, some of which have a *terminus ante quem* because of their deposition in Viking graves in Norway. In particular, comparisons have been cited with sheet-bronze objects decorated with engraved ornament (Bakka 1963, 28–36), such as the *Domnach Airgid* and the Torshov mount.

These monuments from Clonmacnoise and its environs are therefore a closely related local group of sculpture probably produced over a very short space of time. In my view, their somewhat experimental nature and comparisons with Insular manuscripts and metalwork, as well as with sculpture in Scotland, would tend to place them at the beginning of the development of free-standing cross sculpture in Ireland (*pace* Harbison 1992, i, 378–9), and they are certainly earlier than the crosses decorated with predominantly Scriptural iconography.

Acknowledgements

I would like to thank all those who commented on the version of this paper given at the conference at Clonmacnoise, especially Michael Ryan. Illustrations 4–6 and 10–13 are reproduced by kind permission of the National Museum of Ireland. The rest are by the author, and I am grateful to David Thomas for help with the preparation of the photographs for publication.

References

Alexander, J.J.G. 1978 *Insular manuscripts 6th to 9th century*. London.

Allen, J.R. 1896–7 On some points of resemblance between the early sculptured stones of Scotland and Ireland. *Proceedings of the Society of Antiquaries of Scotland* **31**, 309–32.

Allen, J.R. and Anderson, J. 1903 *The early Christian monuments of Scotland* (3 pts). Edinburgh.

Anon. 1951 *Iseal Chiaráin*, the low place of St Ciaran, where was it situated? *Journal of the Ardagh and Clonmacnoise Antiquarian Society*, 52–65.

Bailey, R.N. 1977 The meaning of the Viking Age shaft at Dacre. *Transactions of the Cumberland and Westmoreland Antiquarian and Archaeological Society* **77**, 61–74.

Bailey, R.N. and Cramp, R. 1988 *The British Academy corpus of Anglo-Saxon sculpture, vol. II. Cumberland, Westmoreland and Lancashire North-of-the-Sands*. Oxford.

Bakka, E. 1963 Some English decorated metal objects found in Norwegian Viking graves. *Arbok for Universitet i Bergen, Humanistisk Serie 1*. Oslo.

Bakka, E. 1965 Some decorated Anglo-Saxon and Irish metalwork found in Norwegian Viking graves. In A. Small (ed.), *Proceedings of the fourth Viking congress*, 32–40. London.

Bourke, C. 1986 A panel on the North Cross at Clonmacnoise. *Journal of the Royal Society of Antiquaries of Ireland* **116**, 116–21.

Bréhaut, E. 1912 *An encyclopedist of the Dark Ages: Isidore of Seville*. New York.

Bruce-Mitford, R.L.S. 1960 The Lindisfarne style in metalwork. In T.D. Kendrick *et al.*, *Evangelarum Quattuor Codex Lindisfarnensis*, 250–8. Olten, Lausanne.

Cabrol, F. and Leclercq, H. 1907–53 *Dictionnaire d'archéologie chrétienne et de liturgie*. Paris.

Cooke, T.L. 1853 The ancient cross of Banagher, King's County. *Transactions of the Kilkenny and South-east of Ireland Archaeological Society* **2**, 277–80.

Cramp, R. 1977 Schools of Mercian sculpture. In A. Dornier (ed.), *Mercian studies*, 191–234. Leicester.

Cramp, R. 1978 The Anglian tradition in the ninth century. In J. Lang (ed.), *Anglo-Saxon and Viking Age sculpture*, 1–16. British Archaeological Reports 49. Oxford.

Cramp, R. 1984 *Grammar of Anglo-Saxon ornament, a general introduction to the corpus of Anglo-Saxon stone sculpture*. Oxford.

Crawford, H.S. 1980 *Irish carved ornament* (reprint). Dublin and Cork.

Edwards, N. 1983a Some observations on the layout and construction of abstract ornament in Early Christian Irish sculpture. In H. Thompson (ed.), *Studies in medieval sculpture*, 3–17. London.

Edwards, N. 1983b An early group of crosses from the kingdom of Ossory. *Journal of the Royal Society of Antiquaries of Ireland* **113**, 5–46.

Edwards, N. 1984 Two sculptural fragments from Clonmacnois. *Journal of the Royal Society of Antiquaries of Ireland* **114**, 57–62.

Edwards, N. 1986 The South Cross, Clonmacnois. In J. Higgitt (ed.), *Early medieval sculpture in Britain and Ireland*, 23–48. British Archaeological Reports 152. Oxford.

Edwards, N. 1990 Some crosses of County Kilkenny. In W. Nolan and K. Whelan (eds), *Kilkenny: history and society*, 33–62, 639–44. Dublin.

Gillespie, P. 1918–19 Note on the sculptured figure of a stag on the cross shaft at Clonmacnois, Ireland, in relation to the ancient wooden objects known as otter or beaver traps. *Proceedings of the Society of Antiquaries of Scotland* **53**, 165–7.

Harbison, P. 1992 *The high crosses of Ireland* (3 vols). Bonn.

Henderson, I. 1982 Pictish art and the Book of Kells. In D. Whitelock, R. McKetterick and D. Dumville (eds), *Ireland in early medieval Europe*, 79–105. Cambridge.

Henderson, I. 1987 The Book of Kells and the snake-boss motif on Pictish cross-slabs and the Iona crosses. In M. Ryan (ed.), *Ireland and Insular art A.D.500–1200*, 56–65. Dublin.

Henry, F. 1930 L'inscription de Bealin. *Revue Archéologique* (5 ser.) **32**, 110–15.

Henry, F. 1965 *Irish art in the Early Christian period to 800 AD.* London.

Henry, F. 1974 *The Book of Kells with a study of the manuscript.* London.

Hicks, C. 1980 A Clonmacnois workshop in stone. *Journal of the Royal Society of Antiquaries of Ireland* **110**, 5–35.

Higgitt, J. 1982 The Pictish Latin inscription at Tarbat in Ross-shire. *Proceedings of the Society of Antiquaries of Scotland* **112**, 300–21.

Hillgarth, J.N. 1961–2 Visigothic Spain and Early Christian Ireland. *Proceedings of the Royal Irish Academy* **62C**, 167–94.

Lionard, P. 1961 Early Irish grave slabs. *Proceedings of the Royal Irish Academy* **61C**, 95–169.

Mac Airt, S. and Mac Niocaill, G. (eds) 1983 *The Annals of Ulster to A.D. 1131.* Dublin.

Macalister, R.A.S. 1909 *The memorial slabs of Clonmacnoise, King's County.* Royal Society of Antiquaries of Ireland, additional volume. Dublin.

Macalister, R.A.S. 1949 *Corpus inscriptionum insularum Celticarum*, vol. 2. Dublin.

Mahr, A. 1932 *Christian art in ancient Ireland*, vol. 1. Dublin.

Manning, C. 1992 The base of the North Cross at Clonmacnoise. *Archaeology Ireland* **6** (2), 8–9.

Manning, C. 1994a *Clonmacnoise.* Dublin.

Manning, C. 1994b The earliest plans of Clonmacnoise. *Archaeology Ireland* **8** (1), 18–20.

O'Donovan, J. (ed.) 1856 *Annals of the Kingdom of Ireland by the Four Masters*, vol. 2. Dublin.

Okasha, E. 1971 *Handlist of Anglo-Saxon runic inscriptions.* Cambridge.

Petrie, G. 1872 *Christian inscriptions in the Irish language,* vol. 1 (ed. M. Stokes). Dublin.

Raftery, J. 1941 *Christian art in ancient Ireland*, vol. 2. Dublin.

RCAHMS 1982 *Argyll, Vol. 4. Iona.* Edinburgh.

Ross, A. 1967 *Pagan Celtic Britain.* London.

Ryan, M. (ed.) 1983 *The Derrynaflan hoard I, a preliminary survey.* Dublin.

Ryan, M. 1993 The menageries of the Derrynaflan chalice. In R.M. Spearman and J. Higgitt (eds), *The age of migrating ideas,* 151–61. Edinburgh.

Stevenson, R.B.K. 1955 Pictish art. In F.T. Wainwright (ed.), *The problem of the Picts,* 97–128. Edinburgh.

Stevenson, R.B.K. 1956 The chronology and relationships of some Irish and Scottish crosses. *Journal of the Royal Society of Antiquaries of Ireland* **86**, 84–96.

Stevenson, R.B.K. 1974 The Hunterston brooch and its significance. *Medieval Archaeology* **18**, 16–42.

Stevenson, R.B.K. 1981–2 Aspects of ambiguity in crosses and interlace. *Ulster Journal of Archaeology* **44–5**, 1–27.

Swarzenski, G. 1954 An early Anglo/Irish portable shrine. *Bulletin of the Museum of Fine Arts, Boston* **52**, 50–62.

Wamers, E. 1985 *Insularer Metallschmuck in wikingerzeitlichen Gräbern Nordeuropas Untersuchungen zur Skandinavischen Westexpansion.* Neumünster.

Whitfield, N. 1993 The filigree of the Hunterston and 'Tara' brooches. In R.M. Spearman and J. Higgitt (eds), *The age of migrating ideas,* 118–27. Edinburgh.

Wilson, D.M. 1955 An Irish mounting in the National Museum, Copenhagen. *Acta Archaeologica* **26**, 163–72.

10. ARCHAEOLOGICAL INVESTIGATIONS AT ST CIARÁN'S NATIONAL SCHOOL

Raghnall Ó Floinn and Heather A. King

Abstract

In June 1979 a number of silver coins of Hiberno-Norse type were discovered by schoolchildren in the grounds of St Ciarán's National School during the removal of a set of goalposts. The discovery was reported to the National Museum of Ireland, and Raghnall Ó Floinn carried out an excavation on the site over three and a half weeks in July and August of that year (Part 1; see also Kenny, this vol.).

The second archaeological investigation took place in May 1992 in advance of planning permission being sought by the Department of Education for an extension to the school. No significant archaeological features were uncovered and planning permission was granted. However, having regard to the results of the 1979 excavation and the large area being developed, a monitoring brief was undertaken in March/April 1993 when new ESB cables were brought into the pump-house to the south of the school, and again during the pre-construction phase of works in 1994 (Part 2).

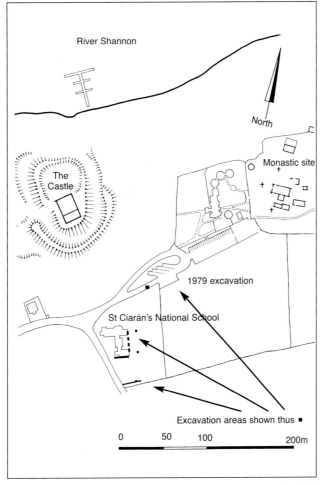

Ill. 1—Location of excavation cuttings at St Ciarán's National School.

PART 1
Raghnall Ó Floinn

Introduction

In June 1979 twelve complete and three fragments of silver coins of Hiberno-Norse type were found in the grounds of Clonmacnoise National School. In view of the possibility of further coins being uncovered and in order to seek to establish a context for the hoard it was decided to carry out limited archaeological excavations on the site.

Ill. 2—View of school grounds from the south, showing location of 1979 excavation cutting (centre).

Excavation

The excavation site was located in the school grounds to the east of the schoolhouse (Ill. 1) and some 200m south-west of the Cathedral. Here the ground slopes gently towards the River Shannon. A cutting measuring 4m x 4m was opened, centred on the post-hole created by the removed goalpost (Ill. 2).

Archaeological deposits in the exposed cutting extended to a maximum depth of 90cm (Ill. 3). The principal features consisted of a series of shallow, parallel-sided drain-like features, U-shaped in cross-section, running north–south and falling with the slope towards the river (Ill. 4). Two of these (F1 and F2), varying in width between 40cm and 50cm and from 20cm to 40cm in depth, were located in the north-western corner of the cutting and ran parallel to one another some 30cm apart. A third (F3), lying some 50cm to the east, was of similar dimensions but contained a large number of boulders. To the east of this lay a series of shallow circular and oval pits and another linear feature (F4) which lay parallel to F1–3. The earliest features found were a circular spread of ash and charcoal (F5) 70cm in diameter located in the south-east of the cutting, and a spread of charcoal (F6) 80cm wide and 1.6m in maximum length which extended from the south baulk. The latter was cut by the stone-lined feature (F3). A sample of charcoal from the spread was identified by Ms M. Scannell of the Herbarium, National Botanic Gardens, as being of oak (*Quercus*). She also identified two seeds found under the charcoal spread as those of hawthorn (*Crataegus*) and

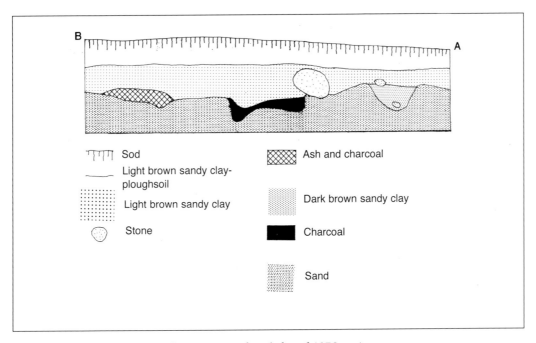

Ill. 3—Section of south face of 1979 cutting.

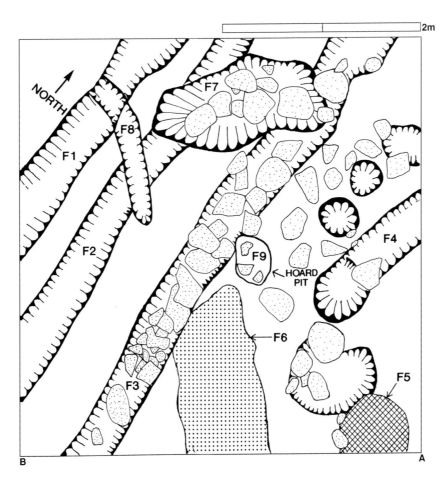

Ill. 4—Plan of 1979 cutting.

Ill. 5—View of 1979 excavation cutting from the south. The hoard pit is located just right of centre.

fumitory (*Fumaria*), the latter being a weed of crops on waste ground.

The parallel-sided features (F1–3) were overlain by two later features—a large oval pit containing boulders (F7), 1.7m in maximum length, 80cm in maximum width and 50cm in maximum depth, and a second, shallow linear feature (F8) overlying F1 and F2 at a diagonal. This measured on average 20cm in width and 15cm in depth.

The original sides of the hoard pit (F9) could not be determined. The oval pit as planned was that of the post-pit dug to take the goalpost and measured 35cm by 45cm (Ill. 5). The digging of the post-pit and the insertion of the goalpost, which measured 18cm in diameter, had displaced the remaining contents of the hoard. A single silver coin was found in ploughsoil about 70cm east of the post-pit. This was of the same type and date as those from the hoard and there is no reason not to regard it as part of the original hoard. Eight silver coins were found in the upper fill of the post-pit. At the lowest level, south of where the goalpost was positioned (and presumably therefore displaced by it), a group of six silver coins fused together were found at a depth of 75cm, and 6cm to the east of these a copper-alloy ingot lay at an angle between 65cm and 70cm in depth. A piece of a twisted gold ornament was found under the position of the goalpost at a depth of 80cm.

The discovery of the single coin in ploughsoil at a distance from the post-pit suggests that the hoard had been disturbed by earlier activity on the site, before the goalpost had been inserted. This suggests that the hoard had been buried at a shallower depth and that the other coins and artefacts found at the base of the post-pit dug for the goalpost (at a depth of between 65cm and 80cm) were driven to a lower depth by the insertion of the post. Because of this the original plan and depth of the pit dug to insert the hoard could not be established, and consequently its relationship with the other features on the site is uncertain.

Finds

Objects from the coin hoard

The excavation uncovered an additional fifteen silver coins (bringing the total to 27 complete and three fragmentary coins), as well as part of an ornament made of twisted gold wire and a copper-alloy ingot (Ill. 6). All the finds from the excavation bear the prefix E181.

The fragment of gold (:1) measures 1.5cm in length, 0.55cm in width, weighs 2.99g, and is cut at one end. It is composed of a band of eight plaited rods which taper towards one end, 0.5cm in maximum diameter, which is folded in two over a thin oblong piece of sheet gold, 0.9cm in length and 0.5cm in width. The outer faces are flattened as if gripped by tongs or pincers.

The dimensions and form of this fragmentary object and the fact that the plaited rods taper towards one end indicate that it originally formed part of an annular plaited-rod gold finger-ring of Viking Age type. Other, complete examples are known from Ireland (Bøe 1940, figs 69–70, 72). These finger-rings may have from three to eight plaited rods which taper towards the ends, where they are linked by a plate, usually lozenge-shaped. The fragment of sheet gold may originally have formed such a plate. According to Graham-Campbell (1995, 55), the simplest (three-rod) plaited finger-rings were introduced to Britain and Ireland during the tenth century, 'but there is no evidence that more complex plaited finger-rings were being produced before the eleventh century'. The

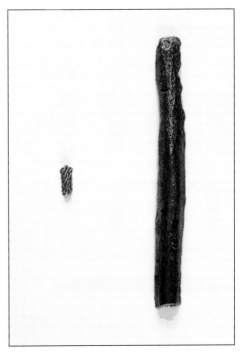

Ill. 6—Gold plaited-rod finger-ring fragment (right) and copper-alloy ingot (left) found with coin hoard.

only ring of this type from a coin hoard is from Soberton, Hampshire, deposited *c.* 1068 (*ibid.*, 55). The coins from the Clonmacnoise hoard, which have been published by Kenny (1983; see also this vol.), are all silver pennies of Hiberno-Norse type. They belong to the latest in the series, and the hoard has been dated to the last decade of the eleventh century or perhaps a little earlier. The fragment of plaited-rod gold finger-ring from the Clonmacnoise hoard therefore fits in well with Graham-Campbell's proposed eleventh-century dating.

The copper-alloy ingot (:2) is of oblong form and D-shaped cross-section with one rounded end, the other cut and broken. Two transverse cuts were made, one from each broad face at an acute angle. Apart from the cuts, the ingot is otherwise unworked and appears fresh from the mould. It measures 13.4cm in length, 1.45cm in width, 1cm in thickness, and weighs 95.04g.

Ingots found in Viking Age hoards are invariably of silver. In shape the ingot is of standard Viking type, found in coin-dated hoards from the ninth to the eleventh centuries. It is, however, not exclusively a Viking type, and copper-alloy examples of oblong, D-sectioned ingots are known from at least the fifth or sixth century from Irish sites such as Garranes, Co. Cork (Youngs 1989, 174), and a crannog at Moylarg, Co. Antrim, where an ingot of copper alloy was found with its stone mould (*ibid.*, 174). Copper-alloy ingots are rare, but stone moulds for producing similar oblong bar-ingots of copper alloy or silver are known from a number of Irish sites, such as Dunbell, Co. Kilkenny, Moynagh Lough, Co. Meath, and St Michael's Hill, Dublin (Armstrong 1920, figs 2 and 3).

The hoard is remarkable for a number of reasons. It is the latest Viking Age hoard from Ireland to contain non-numismatic material and is the only surviving coin hoard to contain artefacts of gold and copper alloy. The fact that both the plaited-rod gold finger-ring fragment and the copper-alloy ingot are cut and the evidence for metalworking in the immediate vicinity (see below) suggest that the hoard may have been part of the stock-in-trade of a goldsmith.

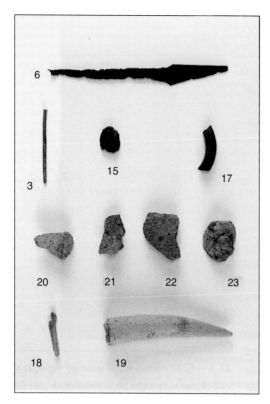

Ill. 7—3: Copper-alloy stick-pin; 6: iron knife; 18: bone needle; 19: worked antler tine; 23: crucible; 20: mould fragment; 21: tuyère; 17: lignite bracelet; 15: chert end scraper.

Other finds

Unless otherwise stated, the other finds were recovered from the light brown sandy clay under the ploughsoil.

Copper alloy

Copper-alloy stick-pin (:3, Ill. 7) with flat nail head, the point missing. L. 5.2cm. It was found just under the topsoil and may therefore be relatively late in date.

Copper-alloy strips (:4, :28, not illustrated).

Iron

Iron knife (:6, Ill. 7) with single edge, straight back and long, tapering tang, slightly recurved at the end. L. 13.3cm. The bent end of the tang suggests that it was inserted into a handle and hammered back. From the ash and charcoal spread (F5).

Iron blade (:12, not illustrated). L. 5.2cm. From the ash and charcoal spread (F5). Possibly part of a draw-knife such as that from Cahercommaun, Co. Clare (O'Neill Hencken 1938, fig. 29, 196).

Iron nails (:7–11, :13, not illustrated). Two of these (:10, :11) were from the ash and charcoal spread (F5) and another (:9) from the charcoal spread (F6).

Iron slag (:26–7, not illustrated). Some 4kg of iron slag was recovered from the cutting, half of this from the topsoil or ploughsoil. One furnace bottom (:27) measuring 12cm in diameter and weighing 0.68kg was found in the oval pit (F7).

Bone

Fragment of bone needle (:18, Ill. 7), comprising part of the head and shank. The head is circular, with a central circular perforation. The shank is circular in cross-section. L. 3.2cm.

Antler tine (:19, Ill. 7), cut at the broader end and faceted. L. 9.2cm, D. 1.9cm. Perhaps an unfinished knife handle.

Baked clay

Portion of a small crucible of grey-white baked clay (:23, Ill. 7) with rounded, in-turned rim; H. 2.8cm, max. T. 0.7cm. The outside is covered with a thick deposit of green dross. Not enough survives to be certain of its original shape, but it may well have been of pyramidal form with triangular mouth (compare Youngs 1989, 180–1).

Two portions of a thick-walled object of baked clay (:21, :22, Ill. 7), vitrified on the outside, which tapers towards the rim. L. of largest 3.3cm; max. T. 1.1cm. The object had a circular opening approximately 3cm in diameter. Its form and dimensions resemble tuyères or blowpipes known from early medieval sites such as Moynagh Lough, Co. Meath (Youngs 1989, 182), or the Brough of Birsay in the Orkney Islands (Curle 1982, ill. 25).

Fragment of fine-grained baked clay (:20, Ill. 7), oxidised a buff colour throughout. This can be identified as part of the valve of a two-piece clay mould. The object is too fragmentary to suggest the type of object which was cast, but a deep, straight impression suggests that it may perhaps have been used to cast the shank of a pin.

Stone

Portion of a lignite bracelet (:17, Ill. 7), D-shaped in cross-section, with an external diameter of *c.* 7cm; W. 0.8cm; T. 0.85cm.

Whetstone fragment (:16, not illustrated), consisting of part of disc with flat, ground broad faces.

A small round scraper of chert (:15, Ill. 7) with secondary retouching on one face; L. 1.9cm; W. 1.5cm; T. 0.65cm. Recovered from topsoil.

Discussion

The cutting was located within the area of the monastic enclosure as suggested by Thomas (1971, 29, fig. 7), although it now appears that the enclosure was more extensive (see Bradley, this vol.). Apart from the coins and the artefacts from the hoard, none of the other finds are diagnostic enough to enable them to be dated. The lignite bracelet and iron knife can be regarded as being of early medieval date. There is no evidence to suggest that there was any prolonged period of activity in the immediate vicinity, and all the finds could date from the eleventh century when the hoard was deposited. The excavated area was not large enough to establish the precise nature of the drain-like features, and the relationship between the hoard and the excavated features could not be determined (see Part 2). The furnace bottom, crucible and tuyère fragments, clay mould fragment and pieces of copper-alloy strips were all found in the north-western quadrant of the cutting, indicating the presence of both ferrous and non-ferrous metalworking in the vicinity. The cut antler tine might represent either an offcut piece or an unfinished artefact such as a knife handle. However, no other pieces of antler were found and it is therefore not possible to suggest that antler-working was practised in the vicinity.

Acknowledgements

I would like to thank the children of St Ciarán's National School, Clonmacnoise, and the late Mr J.J. Walshe, N.T., Principal, who made the discovery of coins at Clonmacnoise; Mr J.D. Delaney of Hodson Bay, Athlone, who made the original report of the discovery to the National Museum; Ms Veronica Baker and Mr Noel Dunne, who assisted in the excavations; and the staff of the National Monuments Service depot, Athenry, for servicing the excavation.

References

Armstrong, E.C.R. 1920 *Guide to the collections of Irish antiquities: catalogue of Irish gold ornaments in the collection of the Royal Irish Academy.* Dublin.

Bøe, J. 1940 *Norse antiquities in Ireland* (= Viking Antiquities in Great Britain and Ireland, Part III). Oslo.

Curle, C.L. 1982 *Pictish and Norse finds from the Brough of Birsay 1934–74.* Society of Antiquaries of Scotland Monograph Series 1. Edinburgh.

Graham-Campbell, J. 1995 *The Viking-age gold and silver of Scotland AD 850–1100.* Edinburgh.

Kenny, M. 1983 A hoard of Hiberno-Norse coins from Clonmacnoise, Co. Offaly. *Numismatic Society of Ireland Occasional Papers* 25, 7–12.

O'Neill Hencken, H. 1938 *Cahercommaun: a stone fort in County Clare.* Dublin.

Thomas, C. 1971 *The Early Christian archaeology of North Britain.* London.

Youngs, S. (ed.) 1989 *'The Work of Angels': Masterpieces of Celtic metalwork, 6th–9th centuries A.D.* London.

PART 2
Heather A. King

Introduction

St Ciarán's National School is situated to the south-west of the monastic enclosure at Clonmacnoise (Ill. 1). The first school on this site was built in 1879 and was slightly further north than the present building. It was replaced in 1948 by the north-west section of the present-day school and enlarged in 1973 by an additional classroom on the south-east (Ill. 8). The 1994 additions to the school involved building two new classrooms which extended *c.* 11m to the east and south of the existing buildings, with two new sumps being dug approximately 8m further to the east in the football field.

The close proximity of the school to the Early Christian monastery on the east and to the Anglo-Norman castle on the north warranted the supposition that settlement evidence from the early and later medieval periods would be located on the site. This supposition was bolstered by the discovery of the Hiberno-Norse coins and the results of Raghnall Ó Floinn's excavation in 1979.

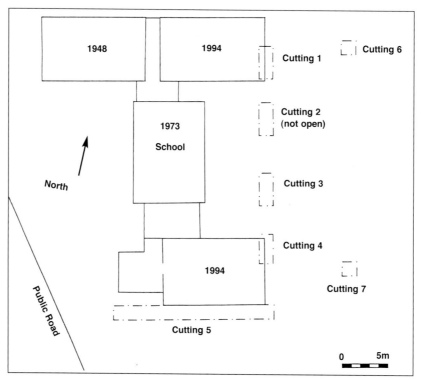

Ill. 8—Plan of new National School and location of cuttings, 1994.

The excavation (Ill. 9)

Initially two cuttings (1 and 4) were seen as being sufficient to assess the archaeological implications of expanding the school, but as these were virtually devoid of any archaeological material a further four cuttings were examined. The cuttings were aligned on the foundation trenches of the proposed new classrooms. Four cuttings (1–4) to the east of the school, two small cuttings in the football field (6 and 7) and one large cutting (5) to the south of the school were, with the exception of Cutting 2, opened, excavated by hand to natural and backfilled.

Cuttings 1 and 3 measured 3.5m north–south by 1.5m east–west; Cutting 2 had the same

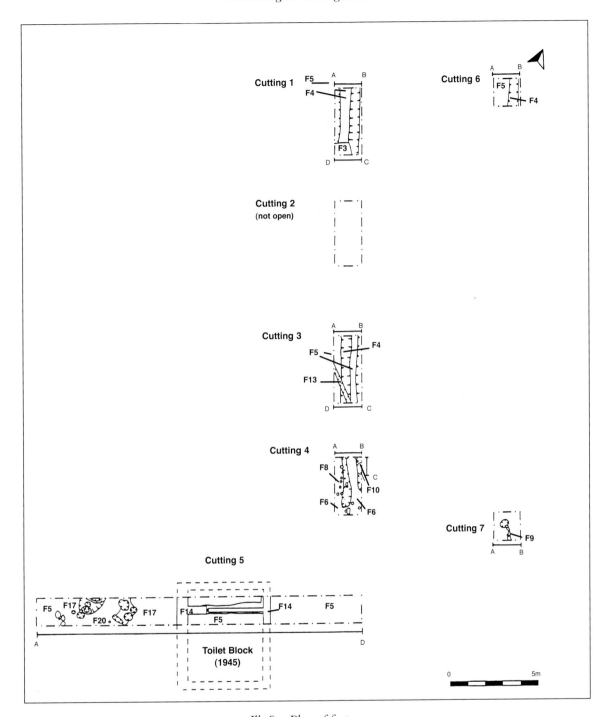

Ill. 9—Plan of features.

dimensions, but apart from stripping the sod no further work was done. Cutting 4 was 3m north–south and 1. 5m east–west. Cutting 5 measured 18m by 1.5m and ran east–west at right angles to Cuttings 1–4. Cuttings 6 and 7 were small cuttings for sumps, 1.5m square. The stratigraphy in all cuttings consisted of a sod *c.* 10–12cm in depth (Ills 10 and 11), underlain by a brown sandy till (F2) *c.* 30cm in depth overlying grey or yellow esker sand (F5). There was evidence below the sod in all cuttings, apart from Cutting 1, of a redeposited layer of soil 4–14cm deep above an earlier sod. Cutting 5 had an additional sticky orange clay (F16) below the sandy till in its eastern half. Cuttings 1, 3, 4 and 6 produced evidence for flattened U-shaped furrows, 40–50cm wide and 30–40cm apart,

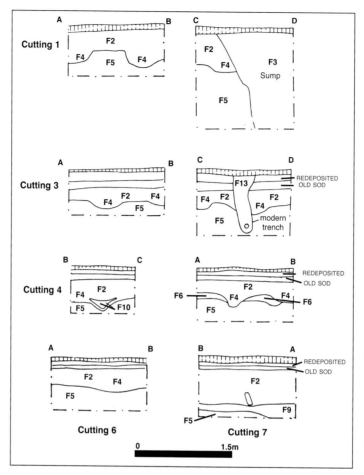

Ill. 10 (above) — Section drawings of cuttings 1, 3, 4, 6 and 7

Ill. 11 (below)— South section of cutting 5

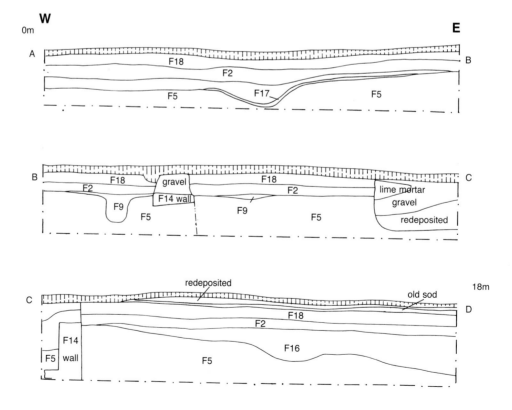

Ill. 12—Cutting 1, showing furrows after excavation.

running north–south (Ill. 12). They were cut into the natural esker deposits at a depth of *c.* 36–48cm and penetrated the natural sands to a depth of 12–14cm. They did not extend to the south baulk of Cutting 4 and were not found in Cuttings 5 and 7.

Modern features included a sump (F3) to drain water from the roof of the school in the south-west corner of Cutting 1, a trench on the west side of Cutting 3 incorporating a plastic pipe bringing water from the pump-house at the south end of the field to a drinking fountain at the side of the school (F13), and a largely forgotten feature in the long east–west Cutting 5 to the south of the school. This feature consisted of a concrete wall (F14) running east–west in the centre of the cutting (Ill. 13). It was located 36cm below the modern surface and was 20cm in width and 68cm in height. It was built with vertical shuttering on a 12cm-high foundation, and both wall and foundation were cut into the grey sand of the esker. The east end of the wall adjoined a north–south wall of the same height but 30cm wide. The west end of the wall was not

dug as deeply and consisted merely of foundations *c.* 10cm deep. This section of the wall was also wider, being 38–43cm wide, and also adjoined a north–south wall *c.* 54cm wide. It was clear that the walls continued to the north and south, and by probing with an iron bar the extent of the structure was determined as being 5m east–west by 5.75m north–south. A 4" concrete block lying on the foundation of the wall suggested a date *c.* 1950 at the earliest (B. Lynch, Irish Cement, pers. comm.). It was also clear from the smooth finish to the top of the wall that the building had been left unfinished, and assessment of the material surrounding the wall suggested that the area had been relatively quickly backfilled.

Subsequently Mr Kieran Mannion, who had worked on the building of the school, was contacted and was able to provide information that the walls represented the foundations of toilets which were planned for the 1948 school. They were abandoned when it was realised that they would have curtailed the size of the football pitch, and new toilets were built at the top (south) of the field beside the fence. The question concerning the shallow foundations at the west end of the building was also resolved. Apparently the contractor was due to arrive earlier than anticipated to inspect the building progress, and

Ill. 13—Cutting 5: F14; foundation wall for 1948 toilet, from east.

Ill. 14—F17 in Cutting 5, from east.

in order to create the impression that the job was further on than it was, a shallow trench was dug and a 'skim' of concrete put in. Following the decision, later that day, to move the toilets, the area was quickly backfilled with material from the alternative foundation trenches. Mr Mannion also supplied information about a large pit (*c.* 3m in diameter) to the south-west of Cutting 5 in which lime mortar for the school was made.

To the west of the 'toilet' block nine shallow pits (F17) were cut into the natural subsoil (Ill. 14) to an average depth of 25cm. A dark brown material lined the pits to a depth of 2cm and covered the ground immediately around them. The function of these pits was unclear, although it was thought possible that they were dug to receive the contents of the dry toilets earlier this century. However, analysis of the material revealed that there was no organic material present and that the brown material was a deposit of manganese leached out of the upper horizons. Three large and two smaller stones lay in the brown sandy soil to the west of the pits but were of no obvious structural significance; there was one post-hole (F20) to the south of the pits, with a diameter of 9cm and a depth of 10cm.

Other features included a series of small stake-holes (F8) on the west side of Cutting 4 (Ill. 9), ranging in diameter from 4cm to 10cm and 2–13cm deep. Some were very shallow (min. depth 2cm) and questionable as stake-holes, but the majority appear to run in a line from north to south and to cut the west edge of the west furrow in the cutting. Two stones on edge were found in this cutting; one lay on top of the fill of the western furrow, and the second lay to the south beyond the limit of the furrow. Two further post-holes were located beneath the latter stone. Within the furrow on the east there was a small pit, 22cm wide and 16cm deep (F10), which had a fill of charcoal and burnt clay (Ill. 10). The charcoal was concentrated at the base of the pit. This pit was not fully excavated as it ran into the east baulk. Although some slag was recovered from near F10 in the eastern furrow it could not be associated with the pit and it was clear that all these features post-date the furrows. A row of four stones on edge (F9) running from the middle of the south baulk and terminating in a shallow pit about midway across Cutting 7 was similarly undatable (Ill. 9).

When construction work commenced, the entire area was stripped of topsoil to a depth of 60–70cm. No features other than the furrows running north–south were noted.

Bowl furnace

In 1993, when a trench was being dug by machine for the insertion of new ESB cabling from the public road to the pump-house along the line of the southern field fence on the west (Ill. 1), a small bowl furnace was uncovered (King 1993b). The trench, *c.* 60cm wide, consisted of 25cm of tarmacadam above natural esker material on the road. Inside the field fence there was 60–70cm of brown sandy soil above natural deposits. Approximately 3m from the road the foundations of the 1950s dry toilets were encountered, and immediately east of these the bowl furnace was uncovered cut into yellow esker sand at a depth of *c.* 80cm (Ill. 15). The cutting was expanded to the north to fully record the furnace, and a

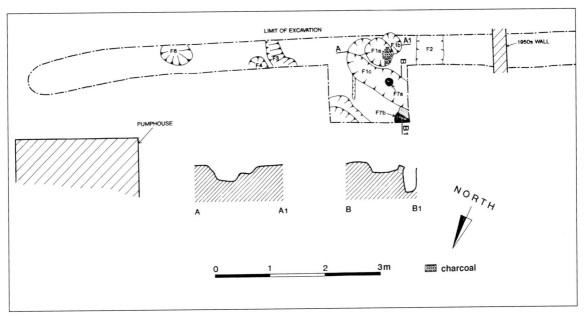

Ill. 15—Plan and section of bowl furnace.

quantity of slag, charcoal, burnt lumps of clay and yellow daub were recovered from the area. The bowl (F1a) was 50cm in diameter with a surviving depth of 30cm. It had a burnt clay lining and was filled with a mixture of brown soil and charcoal. There was a shallow crescent-shaped lip (F1b), *c.* 18cm in depth, on the south-west side, and a trench 52cm wide and 20cm deep encircled the bowl on the east and north and continued downslope to the north-west (F1c). It contained charcoal-flecked brown soil, as did a shallow trench (F2) to the west and Fs 3, 4 and 6 to the east. These were all between 5cm and 8cm deep. Two post-holes (Fs 7a and b) were recorded to the north of the bowl; F7a was 16cm in diameter and 20cm deep, while F7b was 23cm in diameter and 44cm deep.

Finds
The finds were largely modern and were mainly recovered from the brown sandy layer in Cuttings 1–7. They included white and blue wares, brown dairy wares, stoneware, glass, roof tiles, miscellaneous iron nails and fragments, an iron buckle, a 1931 penny, a slate pencil, and clay pipes. A scrap of flint and a flint blade were also recovered. Only a small number of finds hinted at limited archaeological activity in the vicinity of the school: these included a small quantity of animal bone, 2.7kg of slag (92E62:7; not including the slag from the area adjacent to the bowl furnace), a cut antler tip (:16) and a scrap of bronze (:2).

Conclusions
As noted above, there was a considerable amount of relatively modern disturbance around the school and, with the exception of the bowl furnace to the south of the school, there was no evidence for medieval features or finds from the area immediately adjacent to the school. Tillage of uncertain date, but probably relatively modern, was carried out on the east side of the school, but the furrows did not extend to the south of the school. The furrows appear to be similar to those found by Ó Floinn, both in size and orientation, and the evidence suggests that this agricultural activity extended at least as far north and east as Ó Floinn's cutting.

The only evidence for medieval occupation in the area is the apparently isolated occurrence of the bowl furnace and the features in the south and east of Ó Floinn's cutting. The bowl furnace indicates that at least one smith had carried out his iron-smelting activities utilising the shelter provided by the esker ridge and away from dwellings where sparks could cause devastating fires. In any event, it was not used over a long period of time. The features in Ó Floinn's cutting, together with a greater number of medieval finds, other than those found in the hoard pit, appear to suggest a slightly higher level of early medieval activity. However, as Ó Floinn has pointed out (p. 125), there are no grounds for believing that there was substantial or prolonged activity in this area.

The conclusions to be drawn are that the National School area of the monastic site was unoccupied and untilled between the sixth and tenth centuries, although it could have been used for grazing animals. The lack of any depth of stratigraphy in the area, in contrast with that found closer to the monastery, where stratified medieval occupation deposits are on average 1.5m in depth (King 1991–1996; Manning 1986; 1990; 1991), seems to confirm that one is on the edge of the early medieval settlement. The fact that a shallow pit was dug to conceal a hoard of coins and scrap metal might also indicate that the area was on the fringes of the settlement in the eleventh century. It is also important to note that, despite the close proximity of the Anglo-Norman castle, no finds relating to the thirteenth century, when the castle was built and occupied, were found, nor was there any later medieval or post-medieval material recovered.

Acknowledgements

My thanks are due to the school manager, the late Fr Donal Lehane, and the children of St Ciarán's National School, who took a great interest in the excavation. I am particularly grateful to the principal, Mr Liam Broderick, for his interest and cooperation; the assistants on site, Kieran Norton, Liam Darcy and Patrick Anderson; Kieran Mannion for information on the 1948 construction work; Georgia Rennie and Gerard Woods for the finished drawings; Brenda Collins for environmental analysis; and Dr Jim Collins, UCD, for soil analysis. I would also like to thank Declan Ford, Pat Heraghty and his staff of the National Monuments Service for their help and support during the excavation.

References

King, H.A. 1991 'Clonmacnoise New Graveyard', Clonmacnoise. *Excavations 1990*, 49–50. Bray.

King, H.A. 1992 'Clonmacnoise New Graveyard', Clonmacnoise. *Excavations 1991*, 40–1. Bray.

King, H.A. 1993a 'Clonmacnoise New Graveyard', Clonmacnoise. *Excavations 1992*, 53–4. Bray.

King, H.A. 1993b Clonmacnoise. *Excavations 1993*, 67. Bray.

King, H.A. 1994 'Clonmacnoise New Graveyard', Clonmacnoise. *Excavations 1993*, 66–7. Bray.

King, H.A. 1995 New Graveyard, Clonmacnoise. *Excavations 1994*, 74–5. Bray.

King, H.A. 1996 New Graveyard, Clonmacnoise. *Excavations 1995*, 76–7. Bray.

Manning, C. 1986 Clonmacnoise. *Excavations 1985*, 33. Dublin.

Manning, C. 1990 Clonmacnois. *Excavations 1989*, 43–4. Bray.

Manning, C. 1991 Clonmacnoise. *Excavations 1990*, 49. Bray.

11. A HOARD OF HIBERNO-NORSE COINS FROM CLONMACNOISE, CO. OFFALY[*]

Michael Kenny

In May 1979, a group of children changing a goalpost in the playing field of St. Kieran's National School, Clonmacnoise, Co. Offaly, unearthed a number of Hiberno-Norse coins. Their teacher, Mr. J.J. Walshe, reported the find to Mr. James Delaney, the folklore collector who in turn notified the National Museum. An excavation was carried out by Mr. Raghnall Ó Floinn and further coins were recovered, bringing the total to 30 — 27 whole coins and three fragments. Of this total, 12 coins and the three fragments were found by the teacher and pupils and the remaining 15 by Mr. Ó Floinn. Of the latter group nine were scattered loosely and six were stacked together. The excavation of the oval pit in which the coins were buried also yielded a bronze ingot and portion of an ornament made of twisted gold wire.

The hoard is extremely interesting for a number of reasons. Firstly, the fact that a bronze ingot was found with the coins is rather intriguing. In previously documented cases ingots found with Hiberno-Norse hoards have been made of silver. Secondly, coin hoards of the eleventh century (and the one in question could hardly have been deposited before 1095), do not, in the great majority of cases, include ingots at all.

The content of the Clonmacnoise find, therefore, would seem to be somewhat at variance with the general pattern. When we come to the actual coins furthermore this streak of peculiarity is maintained in that only slightly more than half of the pieces are duplicates of previously recorded coins. They are largely Phase III (1035–60) and Phase V (1065–95). A number of them, however, exhibit features and symbols which suggest that they are combinations of Phase II and Phase III. The problem posed by these seemingly contradictory coins is basically whether they are in fact combinations, or later (Phase V) copies of the earlier groups. While it is not possible to come to any definite conclusion on this point, the extent of the blundering of the legends, the execution of the busts and the weight (insofar as it may be used as an indicator) would seem to point towards the later period.

While many of the coins, although not die-duplicates, are easily recognisable in terms of general type, a few are quite unusual and bear only slight resemblance to previously recorded types. Keeping these problems in mind I have attempted to list the coins in groups, beginning with those which are reasonably straightforward and going on to the more difficult pieces. Definite die-duplicates, where given, are noted from the National Museum Collections, which I have been able to study at first hand. In cases where duplicates have been noted in other institutions such as the British Museum or the National Museum, Copenhagen, I have referred to them as 'probable' duplicates for the obvious reason that I have been unable to compare them except photographically. For references to die-duplicates in Belfast, Glasgow and Stockholm, I am indebted to Mr. Wilfred Seaby whose first-hand knowledge of, and familiarity with, Hiberno-Norse coinage in those places, is obviously far superior to my own.

Any attempt to estimate the potential deposition date of this hoard, or the background to its accumulation, is rendered difficult by:

A. the high percentage of coins not previously noted;
B. the combinations of Phase III obverses with Phase II reverses on coins which in

---

★ Reprinted from *Numismatic Society of Ireland Occasional Papers* No. 25 (1983), 7–12.

execution, seem to be Phase V;

C.   the long time-span from the earliest coin (mid Phase III, c. 1040–45) to the latest (possibly the last decade of the eleventh century).

Even if the problematic coins are Phase V copies of earlier pieces, the fact remains that this time-span — probably as much as 60 years — covers two generations.

Two of the coins, however, would seem fairly definitely to suggest a deposition date of c. 1095 at the earliest. No. 18, with its crude rectangular bust, is probably based on the Canopy type or Two Sceptres type of William I (1066–1087). It is not inconceivable that it could have even been inspired by issues of William II (1087–1100).

No. 19, derived from the so-called Agnus Dei issue of Aethelred II, or a Lund penny of Magnus the Good of Denmark (1042–47), is also quite late and is of a type for which Michael Dolley has suggested a date in the early 1090's. A further point of interest is that the reverses of those two coins are identical, suggesting that they were struck around the same time.

This hoard, therefore, is of considerable significance both in terms of its chronological scope and die varieties. In the following list I have attempted to provide such information as may, hopefully, be of some use to those who are involved in studying the coinage of this period.

Moving from numismatics to the broader field of general history, it is worth noting that the period during which the coins were accumulated was one of fairly continuous raiding and plundering throughout much of the country and the monastic settlements seem to have been prime targets for attack. It is not possible to say on what scale this warfare was carried on and the annals which provide us with information must be treated with extreme caution. Since the monasteries were used in some cases as repositories for private posses-sions and as sanctuaries for humans and livestock alike in times of trouble, it is likely that much of their problems stemmed from their involvement, direct or indirect, in local or regional power struggles. While there may be disagreement among historians regarding the scale of those disturbances and their effects upon the lives of the people, there can be little, however, about their frequency. During the period 1044–1106, Clonmacnoise was plun-dered or burned on at least 17 recorded occasions and it is quite likely that there were many minor attacks and disturbances which were not recorded. It is difficult to give dates for these attacks with any certainty, since the annals which are our primary source of informa-tion, are not always in agreement. For example, there were two separate attacks in 1076 and 1078, according to the *Annals of Clonmacnoise*, while the *Annals of the Four Masters* only note one attack in 1077. *The Annals of Clonmacnoise* also refer to an attack by a fleet of ships from Munster in 1090, an attack which is recorded as taking place in 1092 according to the *Annals of Ulster*. Such minor contradictions, however, do not take from the overall picture of uncertainty and, at times, downright chaos. There were, therefore, many occasions dur-ing this period when the necessity to bury coins or other treasure would have arisen. In the light of what I have said already, regarding the possible deposition date of the hoard in ques-tion, it is interesting to note that, after what seems to have been a lull in the 1080's, Clonmacnoise was plundered on at least three occasions in the 1090's — 1090 (or 1092), 1094 and 1098. Although one must be careful not to over-stress the importance of those events, or to make a connection where such may not exist, it is possible that any one of those attacks could have caused the burying of the material. Certainly, if we are to judge from the entries in the annals, it was a time when the soil offered a safer sanctuary for trea-sures than did the monasteries or churches. Another point worth noting is that the frequent attacks on Clonmacnoise were carried out not only by raiders from Munster and Connaught but more often by local septs from its own hinterland — Magawleys, O'Coghlans, O'Breens, O'Melaghlins and slightly further afield, O'Rourkes. Against those local groups, because of their proximity, there could be little forewarning or protection. In such circumstances, the burying of coins and other possessions was probably a fairly frequent operation and a very wise policy.

Works Consulted

Dolley, Michael *The Hiberno-Norse Coins in the British Museum*, (London, 1966). This work is referred to below as "Dolley, *B.M.*".

Dolley, Michael "The Hiberno-Norse Coins without Hoard Provenance in The University Coin Cabinet at Lund" in *Irish Numismatics*, Sept.–Oct. 1978.

Dowle, Anthony & Finn, Patrick *The Guide Book to the Coinage*, (London, 1969).

Galster, Georg *Royal Collection of Coins and Medals, National Museum Copenhagen*, (London, 1979). Referred to below as "Galster, *N.M.C.*"

Graham-Campbell, James "The Viking-age Silver Hoards of Ireland", in *Proceedings of the Seventh Viking Congress*, (Dublin, 1976).

Hauberg, P. *Monetary History of Denmark to 1146*, (Copenhagen, 1900).

Lindsay, John *A view of the Coinage of Ireland from the Invasion of the Danes to the Reign of George IV*, (Cork, 1839).

Lucas, A.T. "The Plundering and Burning of Churches in Ireland, 7th to 16th century" in *North Munster Studies*, (Limerick, 1967).

O'Sullivan, William *The Earliest Irish Coinage*, (Dublin, 1961). Referred to below as "O'Sullivan".

Parsons, Alexander "The Chronology of the Hiberno-Danish Coinage" in *The British Numismatic Journal*, Vol. XVII, 1923–24.

Roth, Bernard "The Coins of the Danish Kings of Ireland. Hiberno-Danish Series" in *British Numismatic Journal*, Vol. VI, 1910. Referred to below as "Roth".

Seaby, Peter *Coins and Tokens of Ireland*, (London, 1970).

Abbreviations

N.M.I. = National Museum of Ireland
U.M.B. = Ulster Museum, Belfast
H.M.G. = Hunterian Museum, Glasgow
R.I.A. = Royal Irish Academy (Coin Collection in N.M.I.)
B.M. = British Museum

Group A — Phase III

Numbers 1–4 have blundered but partly intelligible legends. The features are those of standard Phase III coins — bust to left, plain neck, on the obverse and long cross voided with crescent terminals on the reverse, hands in alternate quarters.

1. *Obv.* + NHNDNF-RIINH. Bust to left, plain neck.
   Rev: +[ΘNΘ NDYFLIN. Hands in alternate quarters.
   Weight .9007 gm.
   Duplicates in N.M.I. — None.
   Duplicates noted by Mr. W. A. Seaby — U.M.B. (2 obv. and 3 rev.); H.M.G. (1 rev.).
   Probable duplicates — Galster, *N.M.C.* no. 114 (obv. and rev.); no. 115 (obv.).

2. *Obv.* + NITRLIFI Λ IDITL. Bust to left, plain neck.
   Rev. —ИI R•I•I BIII[I-II. Hands in alternate quarters.
   Weight 1.1132 gm.
   Duplicates in N.M.I. — R.I.A. no. 3343 (obv. and rev.); R.I.A. no. 3209 (rev.).
   Other duplicates — None known.

3. *Obv.* Ο ⊓I ⊓I⊓ + NDIIIOI. Bust to left, plain neck.
   Rev. + ЛIƎИΟII I Γ II. Hands in alternate quarters.
   Weight .899 gm.
   Duplicates in N.M.I. — None.
   Other duplicates — None known.

4. *Obv.* + И И ⊓ IRII-R DOO. Bust to left, plain neck.
   Rev. •I ⊓II]ИΟIHHИK. Hands in alternate quarters.
   Weight 1.0564 gm.
   Duplicates in N.M.I. — R.I.A. no. 3209 (obv.); Gen. Coll., tray 11, no. 6 (obv.); Stacpoole Coll., H-N Section, no. 49.
   Duplicates noted by Mr. W.A. Seaby — Royal Coin Cabinet, Stockholm. (1 obv. and 1 rev.);
   H.M.G. (1 obv. and 1 rev.).
   Probable duplicates — Galster, *N.M.C.* no. 116 (obv. and rev.). Dolley, *B.M.* no. 84 (obv.); no. 85 (obv. and rev.).

Group B — Phase III

Numbers 5–12 have in common, symbols on the neck and pellets before or behind the bust. The legends are less intelligible than in the previous group, indicating a somewhat later striking date.

5. *Obv.* III⊓IIII⊓II⊓II —— Bust to left, hand on neck. Triangle of pellets in front of nose, large and very faint pellet behind neck.
   Rev. ΟI NIИD II IIII IIIII. Hands in alternate quarters.
   Weight .9689 gm.
   Duplicates in N.M.I. — no. 6 below (obv.);
   Excavations, Medieval Dublin (obv. and rev.).
   Duplicates noted by Mr. W.A. Seaby — U.M.B. (obv. and rev.).
   There is a similar coin, though not a die-duplicate in the N.M.I., R.I.A. no. 3237.

6. *Obv.* Die-duplicate of no. 5 above.
   Rev. ⊙—— (the remainder of the legend is merely a continuation of strokes).
   Weight .8536 gm.
   Duplicates in N.M.I. — no. 5 above (obv.);
   Excavations, Medieval Dublin (obv.); no. 7 below (rev.).
   Duplicates noted by Mr. W.A. Seaby — U.M.B. (obv.).

7. *Obv.* ⊙I——————————— NI. Bust to left, hand on neck. Triangle of pellets in
   front of nose, single pellet at end of legend.
   Rev. Die-duplicate of no. 6 above.
   Weight .8816 gm.
   Duplicates in N.M.I. — no. 6 above (rev.).
   Duplicates noted by Mr. W.A. Seaby — H.M.G. (obv.).

8. *Obv.* ЈIIIIIFIIID [II. Similar to no. 7 above.
   Rev. ⊙ --- (legend of strokes). Hands in alternate quarters.
   Weight .7406 gm.
   Duplicates in N.M.I. — None.
   Very similar to R.I.A. no. 3237.

9. *Obv.* Legend unintelligible. Bust to left, cross patteé on neck. Pellet (and vague
   outlines, possibly of a further two) in front of nose.
   Rev. Legend unintelligible. Hands in alternate quarters.
   Weight 1.0125 gm.
   Duplicates in N.M.I. — None.
   No other duplicates known. There is a general similarity to Dolley, *B.M.* no's
   158–161 (obv.), which would suggest early Phase V rather than late Phase III.

10. *Obv.* Legend unintelligible. Bust to left, cross patteé on neck. Pellet in front of
    nose, two pellets behind neck.
    Rev. Legend unintelligible. Hands in alternate quarters.
    Weight .8937 gm.
    Duplicates in N.M.I. — None.
    No other duplicates known.

11. *Obv.* NIIHIII[ININI⊙. Bust to left, cross patteé on neck. Pellet in front of nose,
    two pellets behind neck.
    Rev. INI-IIHIOIMI INN. Hands in alternate quarters. Very faint outline of pellet
    in one quarter.
    Weight 1.0037 gm.
    Duplicates in N.M.I. — R.I.A. no's 3223-5 (obv.);
    Excavations, Medieval Dublin (obv.); R.I.A. no. 3224 (rev.).
    Duplicates noted by Mr. W.A. Seaby—U.M.B. (1 obv.); H.M.G. (5 obv. and 2 rev.);
    Isle of Man, private coll. (1 obv.).
    Probable duplicates — Dolley, *B.M.* no. 133; Galster, *N.M.C.*, no. 219.
    This particular variety has been noted and discussed by Michael Dolley in *Irish
    Numismatics*, Nov.–Dec., 1979, and by W.A. Seaby in the same journal,
    March–April, 1980.

12. *Obv.* +IOIN NICILE. Bust to left, symbol (loop enclosing pellet) on neck. Pellet in front of nose.
    Rev. NINNININ   TICN. Hands and pellets in alternate quarters.
    Duplicates in N.M.I. — None.
    Other duplicates — None known.
    The obverse, with its rather odd symbol on the neck is similar to N.M.I., R.I.A. no's 3248 and 3350; Lindsay, Plate 3, no. 61; Galster, *N.M.C.*, no. 256; a coin in the University Coin Cabinet at Lund, noted by Michael Dolley in *Irish Numismatics*, Sept.–Oct., 1978.

Group C — Phase V

Numbers 13–16 below have symbols on the neck and pellets around the bust rather like those of the preceding group. They have a distinctive reverse, however — pellet, annulet, pellet and anchor, in the angles of the cross. This would seem to indicate a similarity with some coins of the Kirk Michael (Isle of Man) hoard (Dolley, *B.M.* no's. 157–162).

13. *Obv.* Legend unintelligible. Bust to left, cross on neck. Two pellets in front of nose, four pellets, diamond-shape, behind neck.
    Rev. Legend unintelligible. Pellets in opposite quarters, anchor and annulet in remaining quarters.
    Weight .875 gm.
    Duplicates in N.M.I. — no. 14 below (obv.).
    Other duplicates — None known. Very similar reverse to Dolley, *B.M.* no's. 157–162.

14. *Obv.* Die duplicate of no. 13 above.
    Rev. Legend unintelligible. Similar to no. 13 above.
    Weight .741 gm.

15. *Obv.* Legend unintelligible. Bust to left, cross on neck. Three pellets, partly joined, in front of nose, two pellets behind neck.
    Rev. Legend unintelligible. Similar to no's. 13–14.
    Weight .881 gm.
    Duplicates in N.M.I. — None.
    Other duplicates — None known.

16. *Obv.* Legend unintelligible. Bust to left, symbol (rather like small case, retrograde 'F') on neck. Two pellets in front of nose, four pellets, diamond-shape, behind neck.
    Rev. Legend unintelligible. Similar to no's. 13–15 above.
    Weight .607 gm.
    Duplicates in N.M.I. — None.
    Other duplicates — None known.

Group D — Phase V

Numbers 17–19 are the only coins in this hoard which do not have the left-facing bust on the obverse and are arguably the most interesting.

17. *Obv.* Legend unintelligible. Facing bust with helmet and cloak.
    Rev. Legend unintelligible. Unidentified symbol in one quarter.

Weight .898 gm.
Duplicates in N.M.I. — None.
Other duplicates — None known. Similar coins include O'Sullivan no. 44 and
Dolley, *B.M.,* 188-92.

18. *Obv.* Legend unintelligible. Facing bust, crude and rectangular in shape. Very
noticeable ears (rather like cup handles).
Rev. Legend unintelligible. Symbol (dagger, sword or sceptre) in one quarter.
Weight .7006 gm.
Duplicates in N.M.I. — no. 19 below (rev.).
Other duplicates — None known.

19. Obv. Legend unintelligible. Animal (*agnus dei?*) facing left, pellets on forequarters
and under neck. Large pellet for eye. Cross over back and, above, two hands
reaching downwards and outwards.
Rev. Die duplicate of no. 18 above.
Duplicates in N.M.I. — no. 18 (rev.).
Other duplicates — None known. Similar to N.M.I., R.I.A. no. 3389 (obv.);
U.M. no. 333 (C–B) (obv.); Roth, no's. 182–183.

Group E — combinations of Phase II and Phase III

The following coins are somewhat problematic in that they portray features associated
with Phase II and Phase III, although their crude execution would seem more in keeping
with Phase V.

20. *Obv.* Legend unintelligible. Crude bust to left, hand on neck. Cross pommée in
front of nose, triangle of pellets at tip of nose, single pellet at end of legend.
Rev. Legend unintelligible. Tiny pellet in each quarter.
Weight .7729 gm.
Duplicates in N.M.I. — None.
Other duplicates — None known.

21. *Obv.* Legend unintelligible. Similar to no. 20 above.
Rev. ΘIIII IINI IDII. Similar to no. 20 above.
Weight .9003 gm.
Duplicates in N.M.I. — R.I.A. no. 3140 (obv. and rev.). The R.I.A. coin was
noted by Roth and listed no. 60 in his work.

22. *Obv.* Legend unintelligible. Similar to no's 20–21.
Rev. Legend unintelligible. Similar to no's 20–21.
Weight .5083 gm.
Duplicates in N.M.I. — no. 23 below (obv. and rev.).

23. *Obv.* Die duplicate of no. 22.
Rev. Die duplicate of no. 22.
Weight .504 gm.
Duplicates in N.M.I.—no. 22 (obv. and rev.).
Other duplicates—None known.

24. *Obv.* Legend unintelligible. Plain neck, symbol (sceptre and annulet?) behind neck.
    Rev. Legend unintelligible. Similar to no's. 20–23.
    Weight .914 gm.
    Duplicates in N.M.I. — None.
    Other duplicates — None known.

25. *Obv.* Legend unintelligible. Badly struck.
    Rev. Legend unintelligible. Similar to no's 20–24.
    Weight .96 gm.

26. *Obv.* Legend unintelligible. Large bust, three small pellets high on neck.
    Rev. Legend unintelligible. Hand in one quarter, pellets in three quarters.
    Weight .8167 gm.
    Duplicates in N.M.I. — None.
    Other duplicates — None known.

27. *Obv.* Legend unintelligible. Bust to left, plain neck, two pellets in front of nose, one pellet at end of legend.
    Rev. Legend unintelligible. Similar to no. 26.
    Weight .8685 gm.
    Duplicates in N.M.I. — None.
    Other duplicates — None known.

28a. (Fragment).
    Obv. Legend unintelligible. Bust to left, vague outline of symbol (cross pommée) in front of nose.
    Rev. Legend unintelligible. Pellets in three quarters (fourth missing).

28b. (Fragment).
    Half of coin missing. Probably Phase III or V.

28c. (Fragment).
    Half of coin missing. Probably Phase III or V.

Ill. 1a and b—Obv. and rev.

Ill. 2a and b—Obv. and rev.

Ill. 3a and b—Obv. and rev.

Ill. 4a and b—Obv. and rev.

Ill. 5a and b—Obv. and rev.

Ill. 6a and b—Obv. and rev.

Ill. 7a and b—Obv. and rev.

Ill. 8a and b—Obv. and rev.

Ill. 9a and b—Obv. and rev.

Ill. 10a and b—Obv. and rev.

Ill. 11a and b—Obv. and rev.

Ill. 12a and b—Obv. and rev.

Ill. 13a and b—Obv. and rev.

Ill. 14a and b—Obv. and rev.

Ill. 15a and b—Obv. and rev.

Ill. 16a and b—Obv. and rev.

Ill. 17a and b—Obv. and rev.

Ill. 18a and b—Obv. and rev.

Ill. 19a and b—Obv. and rev.

Ill. 20a and b—Obv. and rev.

Ill. 21a and b—Obv. and rev.

Ill. 22a and b—Obv. and rev.

Ill. 23a and b—Obv. and rev.

Ill. 24a and b—Obv. and rev.

Ill. 25a and b—Obv. and rev.

Ill. 26a and b—Obv. and rev.

Ill. 27a and b—Obv. and rev.

Ill. 28a —Obv. and rev.

Ill.28b—Obv. and rev.

Ill. 28c—Obv. and rev.